S. H. Platt

Christian Holiness

S. H. Platt

Christian Holiness

ISBN/EAN: 9783743467736

Manufactured in Europe, USA, Canada, Australia, Japa

Cover: Foto ©Lupo / pixelio.de

Manufactured and distributed by brebook publishing software (www.brebook.com)

S. H. Platt

Christian Holiness

CHRISTIAN HOLINESS:

ITS

Philosophy, Theory, and Experience.

BY REV. S. H. PLATT, A.M.,

AUTHOR OF

"*The Gift of Power;*" "*Christ and Adornments;*" "*The Philosophy of Christian Holiness;*" "*Christian Separation from the World;*" "*The Man of Like Passions;*" "*The Christian Law of Giving;*" "*To Every Man His Work;*" "*My 25th Year Jubilee;*" "*The Power of Grace;*" "*The Wondrous Name;*" "*Queenly Womanhood;*" "*Princely Manhood;*" "*Nevertheless;*" "*Heredity.*"

BROOKLYN, N. Y.:
THE HOPE PUBLISHING COMPANY,
1882.

PREFACE.

Books, like men, have a history. The origin of this volume was in a hastily prepared sermon preached at the Messiah Camp-meeting at Milford, Conn., Sept. 1, 1865, which, at a special meeting of the ministers present was requested for publication. Upon being printed in pamphlet form, the whole edition of 2300 copies was sold within a few days.

Bishop R. S Foster, in his revised edition of "*Christian Purity*," did it the honor to quote entire thirty-four of its thirty-seven pages, with mingled approbation and dissent, concluding with this paragraph: "The treatise contains not only important and astutely expressed truth, but more than that, points the way to some deep and occult cases which are of real value to the discussion. With slight verbal changes and a few modifications of ideas, we should feel that the treatise is not only able, but essentially correct. It has three great merits; its spirit is excellent, its manner is fresh and unique, and it recognizes and enforces the great doctrine of the need and possibility of advanced holiness on the part of believers; not failing to recognize the fact that the Holy Ghost is the great agent who also will do it in a moment on the faith of the seeking soul." "*Christian Purity*," pp. 363-4.

Much thought and frequent intercourse with seekers after the higher grades of Christian experience, together with a free interchange of views with many who have experienced much, have convinced the writer of the need of a work upon this subject differing in its forms of statement, scope of application and clearly defined limitations, from all that has previously appeared. Ignoring no well-established facts, controverting no class of writers, seeking nothing new because it is new, clinging to nothing old because it is old, but prayerfully appropriating all helps of science within reach, and fearlessly expressing facts of Christian experience in terms of modern thought, the writer has endeavored to evolve something that shall help the struggling spirit in its efforts to reach higher good; (whether he has succeeded in retaining the excellences above named, the reader will decide.) In doing so, he has felt the impulse of a profound conviction that every branch of human knowledge is susceptible of philosophical treatment, and that whenever a sufficient number of facts have been noted to justify that attempt, a candid and patient effort in that direction will always be productive of good.

"Let there be laid before the Church, especially before souls panting after, 'all the fullness of God,' the exact transcript of each Christian consciousness under the illumination of the Holy Ghost, so far as language can be a vehicle of that which 'passeth knowledge,' and not only will souls in trouble be comforted, but there will be accumulated a mass of facts, out of which some analytical mind, some theological Sir William Hamilton, may do what all systemizers have hitherto failed to do, construct out of the Bible and experience, a consistent and symmetrical science of Christian perfection." *Rev. Daniel Steele, D. D.*

The Author is not vain enough to believe himself the Sir Wm. Hamilton referred to, but consoles himself with the thought that when that Philosopher does appear he will not be unwilling to have had his work pioneered by even this small effort in the direction of systematic statement.

As to the success of the present undertaking it is for one class of readers only to decide, viz., those who will survey its several parts, not as detached statements isolated from their relations, but as segments of the one whole, and that whole to be carefully considered in the spirit of investigation which discards all prejudice and holds all theories in check while the examination proceeds.

Such as it is, it is trustfully committed to the care of that Providence who will assign its sphere and guard its results. THE AUTHOR.

MY WORK.

Hast thou work for me, my Father,—
  Work for me, and me alone?
Task thou canst not give another,—
  Let that task to me be shown.

Does that deed to me, my Father,
  Seem so little and unknown
That, to greater I would rather
  Turn and leave this all undone?

Hast *such* work for me, my Father,
  Work that should this day be done—
From some field a sheaf to gather?
  Now I make that work my own.

Hast thou work for me, my Father,
  Work to large dimensions grown?
For that toil of faith and power
  Now anoint thy trusting one.

Come, my Father, strong and loving,
  Guide and Helper, kind and true,
To my heart this moment proving
  Thou dost give the power to do.

O, my Father, in my doing
  Let thy will be fully done!
May that will—divine, unerring,
  Crown the work by me begun.

TABLE OF CONTENTS.

PART I. ITS PHILOSOPHY.

CHAPTER I. THE LEGITIMATE SCOPE OF THE SUBJECT.

1. Not to prove its existence. p. 1
2. Not to correct theological misstatements of it.
3. Must survey all classes of facts pertaining to it. pp. 2, 3.
4. Should exhibit the principles in accordance with which the experience becomes possible. p. 4.
5. Should consider the forces involved, as deducible from its facts and principles. p. 4.
6. Must enunciate the laws of the subject. p. 4.
7. Should show the relation of those laws to the facts of personal responsibility. p. 5.

CHAPTER II. THE EXPERIMENTAL FACTS STATED. P. 6.

1. Pre-regenerate. pp. 6–17. 1. A universal consciousness of guilt. p. 6. 2. A corruption of the Nature. p. 7. (1) Original. p. 7–9. (2) Acquired. p. 9. A. Physical. p. 10. B. Mental. p. 10. C. Spiritual. p. 10. (3) Hereditary. pp. 11–14. 3. Contrition for sin. (1) Self-condemnation. p. 15. (2) Grief. p. 15. 4. Repentance for sin. p. 16. 5. Belief in Christ as a present Savior. p. 17. (1) Intellectual credence. (2) Hearty reliance.
2. Con-regenerate facts. p. 18. 1. A mysterious internal change—embracing. (1) An assurance of pardon. (2) A consciousness of freedom from guilt. (3) The absence of self-condemnation. p. 19. (4) Consciousness of love for God and his people. (5) Absolute and grateful submission to all his will. (6) A new-born zeal to do good. p. 20. (7) Hatred of sin. (8) Joy in the Holy Ghost. p. 21. 2. An outward change corresponding with the inward.

3. Post-regenerate facts. p. 22. 1. A period of joyful triumph. 2. A sad discovery of in-dwelling sin. 3. Consternation and confusion. p. 23. 4. Rallying to the struggle. p. 24. 5. Alternate victories and defeats. 6. The cleansing. p. 25. 7. The re-awakenings. p. 27. 8. The renewed cleansings.

CHAPTER III. THE FORCES ENGAGED. P. 28.

Spirit, soul and body discriminated. p. 29. Attributes of each. pp. 29, 30. The difference. p. 30. Spirit faculties of a higher order. Spirit has three that the soul has not. pp. 31, 32.

1. Spirit-forces. Divine; human; Satanic. p. 33.
2. Psychical,—soul-forces involved.
3. Physical. 1. Vital force. 2. Sensibility-co-operating force. p. 34. 3. Automatic, or reflex activity force. The law of spirit-habit. p. 34. Habit. p. 35. 4. Will-co-operating force. 5. Mind-conditionating force. The structure and function of the brain and nerves. p. 36. The cerebro-spinal nervous system. p. 36. Two kinds of tissue in nervous system. p. 37. (1) White substance. (2) Grey substance. The structure of nerve filaments. p. 38. A. Colorless tubular membrane. B. Semi-fluid tubular marrow. C. Axis cylinder. The cerebro-spinal system consists of—p. 39—A. The spinal cord. B. The medulla oblongata. p. 40. C. The sensory ganglia. D. The cerebellum. E. The cerebrum. Their appliances for the discharge of their functions are: A. The spinal cord and its thirty-two pairs of nerves. p. 40. The functions of the cord are, (a) That of a nerve-center. pp. 41, 42. With a triple object, viz.: ((a)) To scatter an entering influence into a number of tracks. p. 43. ((b)) To combine it into a new result. ((c)) To retain a residuum from it. (b) Another function of the cord is as a nerve of communication. p. 44. (c) Still another is as a pathway for certain channels of sensation. The medulla. p. 44. Sensorium-commune. p. 45. Conscious sensations. Reflex actions. Involuntary movements. May be

excited by the organic stimuli. p. 46. Consciousness. p. 47. The sensory ganglia are, p. 48. (1) Seats of sensational consciousness. (2) Of consciousness of mental states. (3) Centres of sensori-reflex movements. (4) Springs of nervous force to bear the mandates of the will to the muscles. The cerebellum,—co-ordinates voluntary movements. p. 49. The cerebrum receives impressions from the immaterial spirit. p. 49. The will of the spirit stands in the place of a higher nervous centre. pp. 49–50. The direction of the reactions of the cerebrum. p. 51. The nature of emotions. p. 51. Determined largely by the acquired nature. p. 52. The psychical tone. p. 52. The will in some relations automatic. p. 53.

CHAPTER IV. THE PRINCIPLES CONCERNED. P. 55.

1. Those which relate to God. 1. God's equity in grace. p. 56. 2. Different degrees of moral purity consistent with a Christian character. p. 57. 3. The incompatibility of present justification with a present state of moral unfitness for heaven. p. 59. 4. Holiness the grand requisite for admission to heaven. p. 61. How much? p. 62. (1) So much as is involved in regeneration. (2) Such as is added by a faithful life. (3) Such as is given in the hour of death. No promise of such. p. 63. Reasons against the view. pp. 63–67. 5. The immediate accomplishment of His part of the work of salvation upon the occurrence of the right conditions in the subject. p. 67. 6. The necessity of dealing with dissimilar facts as dissimilar. p. 68. The me and the my.

2. Principles which relate to men. p. 70. Preliminary propositions. First—Religious mental processes subject to the ordinary laws of mental action. p. 70. Second—Physical states modify mental action in religious experience. 1. He must be convicted of the reality and malignity of his moral disease. p. 71. 2. Must be convinced that there is an effectual

remedy for him. 3. Must desire and determine to procure it. 4. Must be conscious of the validity of his efforts. p. 72. 5. Must have a positive assurance of cure. 6. Yet all these things subject to the modifications induced by physical conditions. p. 73.
3. Principles which relate to the Tempter. 1. Unmitigated hostility to the work in all its phases. p. 73. 2. Pre-inclination to frustrate it. p. 74.

CHAPTER V. THE LAWS IN ACTION. P. 74.

1. *Mental.* p. 75. 1. Laws of normal development and action. (1) The recognized dominancy of reason, conscience and judgment. (2) Each faculty used in its own sphere. p. 76. (3) The testimony of each unimpeachable within its appropriate sphere. p. 77. 2. Laws of abnormal development and action. p. 78. (1) Perversity:—regulative faculties overborne. Illustrations of its power. Habits. Coleridge. pp. 79-81. Largely physical. pp. 81-82. (2) Irregularity:—habitual disuse, or excessive use of certain faculties.
2. *Spiritual.* 1. Laws of normal spiritual development and action. p. 85. (1) Acceptance of Christ as the all-sufficient Savior. (2) Complete submission to the will of God. p. 85. (3) Entire consecration to the work of God. (4) Reliance upon the guidance and sustainment of the Holy Spirit. p. 87. (5) Procurement of the special helps of grace. 2. Laws of abnormal spiritual development and action. p. 88. (1) Partial acceptance of Christ. (2) Rebellion against God's will. p. 89. (3) Defective consecration to God's work. (4) Partial self-guidance and self-dependence. p. 90. (5) Neglect of the aid of the Holy Spirit. (6) Mental instability. (7) Excessive mental bias. p. 91. (8) Bodily infirmities.
3. *Physical.* p. 92. 1. Laws of normal development and action. (1) Healthful respiration. (2) Normal circulation. (3) Adequate and balanced nutrition. p. 93. (4) Well-regulated activity. (5) Timely

CONTENTS. xi.

and sufficient protection. 2. Laws of abnormal development and action. (1) Disturbance of function. p. 94. A. Diminished or excessive functional activity. B. Sympathetic disturbance of other functions. (2) Organic change of functional product. p. 95. (3) Consequent organic changes elsewhere. (4) Inheritance. p. 96. Heredity defined. Physical and moral degeneracy the result. p. 97. Deviations from the normal type. p. 98. The habit of the parent becoming the instinct of the child. Intemperance and insanity. p. 99. Moral liberty. p. 100. *The laws of transmission and heritage.* p. 101. A. Uniformity. B. Duplication. a. Physical peculiarities of structure or functions. pp. 102-104. b. Organic or nervous diseases. p. 104. c. Special tendencies or aptitudes to certain modes of action. p. 104. d. Mental traits. p. 105. e. Sentiments and passions. C. Diversity. a. In species and varieties. p. 107. b. In nervous diseases. p. 108. c. In the transmission of temporary states. p. 109. D. Impressional heredity. p. 110-114. E. Recurrency. p. 114. *Modifying forces.* p. 115. a. The influence of one parent in counteracting that of the other. p. 116. b. The union of the influence of both. c. Any influence that gives temporary dominancy to the forces of diversity as against duplication, and vice versa. p. 117. d. Any habitual subjection to cause that antagonize recurrency. e. Spontaneous variations. *The cause of transmission.* p. 119. Heredity as related to the temperaments, viz.: inactive, vital, mental. p. 121.

CHAPTER VI. THE RELATION OF THESE LAWS TO PERSONAL RESPONSIBILITY. P. 123.

1. Personal responsibility is modified by two principles. 1. Sufficient knowledge. 2. Sufficient power. p. 124.
2. These principles applied. p. 125. 1. Sufficiency of knowledge. 2. Sufficiency of power. p. 126. A

distinct species of abnormal humanity. p. 127. (1) A condition in which impulse is the only law. p. 128. (2) May be induced by circumstances. (3) Their responsibilty. The chemistry of character. pp. 129–131. Special laws for the unfortunates. p. 131. (1) Conscious integrity of purpose. (2) Honest and habitual effort to carry it out. p. 132.
3. With sufficient knowledge and power the normal laws of Christian holiness sweep through the entire field of personal responsibility. pp. 132–134. So of the normal laws of physical action. pp. 134–136.

PART II.

CHAPTER I. THE THEORY OF CHRISTIAN HOLINESS. P. 136.

1. Man has a three-fold nature.
2. Spirit discriminated from soul.
3. Conscience, intuitions, and moral obligation.
4. Conscience demands perfect obedience.
5. Intelligence apprehends a law of obedience and a future existence.
6. Depravities.
7. Plan of grace.
8. After regeneration depravities inhere in the soul and body. p. 138.
9. Proper work of Christian life is to—1. Continue regenerated. 2. Seek the complemental condition of soul and body. 3. Complimental condition reached by—(1) Substituting out. (2) Revolutionary power of the Holy Spirit. 4. Complimental condition maintained.
10. Power of the Holy Spirit in the expulsion of acquired appetites, &c. p. 139.
11. In the cure of diseases. pp. 140-142.
12. Natural appetites readjusted. pp. 142-143.
13. The modus operandi. p. 144.
14. The law of emotion. p. 145.
15. Transmission of godly predispositions. p. 146.
16. Possible sanctifications. p. 148. 1. Normal. 2.

Neuropathic. 3. Super-normal. 4. Emotional
17. Interchangeable. p. 149.
18. Outward evidences. p. 149. 1. Normal; harmony with the will of God. 2. Neuropathic; wanting. 3. Super-normal; a marked contrast in addition to the normal evidence. p. 150.
19. These discriminations must be made in the interests of large-hearted charity.

CHAPTER II. OBJECTIONS CONSIDERED. P. 152.

1. To assumed facts. 1. To the reality of any such experience as Christian Holiness. 2. To the underlying assumption that consciousness correctly reports the true state of the heart. p. 153. 3. To the assumption that Christians are not made entirely holy by a single act of sanctifying grace. p. 154. 4. To the assumption that Philosophy is competent to deal with this question without the aid of Revelation. p. 156.
2. Verbal objections. "The phraseology is unusual, and will not be understood." p. 157.
3. Logical objections. p. 158. 1. "Too much concession made to the materialistic theories of the day." 2 "Free-will is limited in the ratio of the extension of heredity." p. 159. 3. "Education is more powerful than heredity." p. 161. 4. This use of heredity loads parents with a responsibility fearful to contemplate. p. 162.
4. Theoretical objections. 1. "The classification of sanctification gives too much ground to self-exculpation." p. 163. 2. "In attributing depravity to the soul and body, the Scriptures are denied and a doctrine of heathen philosophy is foisted into Christianity." p. 164. 3. "The eradication of artificial appetites is a delusion." p. 166. 4. "The doctrine of faith-cures has no foundation in fact in these times, and tends to fanaticism." pp. 167-170. 5. "The supposition on page 144 that brain and nerves are subject to spirit influence has no foundation." p. 170. 6. "Too much stress is laid upon the sug-

gestions of the Holy Spirit." p. 172. 7. "There is nothing in the Bible about peculiar constitutions." p. 175. 8. "There are remnants of the old depravity existing after regeneration." p. 176.

PART III. THE EXPERIENCE. P. 178.

Chapter 1. Practical Deductions. P. 179.

1. Explanatory of the way. 1. A way of positive self-assertion. 2. Of the highest self-abnegation. p. 180. 3. Of entire consecration. p. 182. 4. Of invincible resolution. p. 183. 5. Of unquestioning faith. p. 185. Involving certain elements. pp. 186–192. 6. Of immovable trust. p. 192. 7. Of determined avoidance of the abnormal. p. 194–199.
2. Advisory as to the methods. p. 200. 1. Make right discriminations as to what is required. (1) Exact correspondence of real with ideal Christian life not expected. (2) Conscious environment of Deity "*keeping*" the soul not looked for. p. 202. (3) Constant stretch after the higher not desirable. p. 203. (4) Complete control of the thoughts not to be hoped for. p. 204. Effects of accidents and diseases detailed. pp. 204–213. Criterion to distinguish the genesis of thoughts. p. 214. (5) The experience is not an undisturbed calm. p. 214. (6) It does not imply the absence of painful and unreasonable emotions. p. 215. (7) Freedom from peevish tempers not to be looked for. p. 218. (8) Absence of sense-deceptions not involved. p. 221. (9) Extinguishment of morbid appetites not implied. p. 222. (10) Control of nervous agitations not supposed. p. 223. (11) Absence of spasmodic muscular movements not involved. p. 224. *What then is involved?* p. 224. 1. Not to attempt the impracticable. 2. Rightly distribute the work to be done. p. 225. 3. Do your part faithfully. p. 226. 4. Trust God to do his part instantly. p. 226.

3. Admonitory of the dangers. p. 227. 1. Dallying with temptation. 2. Resting in partial success. p. 229. 3. Suppression of testimony. 4. Repression of the emotions. p. 230. 5. Seeking a quiescent peace. p. 233. 6. Fanaticism. p. 235. 7. Canting pietism.

CHAPTER II. THE SUBJECT PRACTICALLY APPLIED.

1. *To the private Christian.* p. 235. 1. As an experience personally needed. 2. As an experience certainly attainable. p. 237. An experience traced. pp. 238-240. Grace sanctifies just as far as the will definitely concurs. p. 241. Illustrated by blood disease. p. 242. Habits may be eradicated in two ways— (1) By voluntary, gradual obliteration and substitution. p. 244. Subject to—a. The law of impression. b. The law of inspiration. p. 245. (2) By revolutionary and supernatural substitution. p. 246. Illustrative examples. Must be preceded by consecration. p. 249. 3. As peculiarly affecting the marriage relation. p. 250. Duty of parents to beget children better than themselves.
2. The subject applied to organized churches. p. 254. 1. As a formula of faith. (1) The creed of limited salvation. (2) The creed of holiness. p. 255. 2. As the mightiest force of evangelism. p. 256. Sanctified men are God's veterans. p. 258. Conductors of Omnipotence. p. 260. The endowments of power. p. 261. Illustrative examples of. pp. 265-271.
3. The subject applied to the ministry. p. 271. 1. As a source of personal and pulpit power. Example. The philosophy of the matter. p. 273. The types of the old dispensation. p. 274. Ministers are sample-exhibitors. p. 276. 2. As a means of revival interest. p. 278. Purity has the maximum of constitutional spontaneities and the minimum of clogging antagonisms. p. 279.
4. The subject applied to the press. p. 281. 1. As a standard of public morality. 2. As a reformatory agency among men. p. 282.

5. The subject applied to institutions of learning. p. 284. 1. As crowning culture with the glory of purity. 2. As approximating the attainable perfection of man. p. 286. 3. As giving such institutions the moulding power that they ought to possess. p. 287.

CHRISTIAN HOLINESS:

Its Philosophy, Theory, and Experience.

CHAPTER I.

THE LEGITIMATE SCOPE OF THE SUBJECT.

1. It is no part of the philosophy of a thing to prove its existence.

Therefore, the present treatise will assume the fact of Christian Holiness without argument, and will have no concern with the difficulties or objections grounded upon a denial of that state of grace.

2. It is not designed to correct theological misstatements of the doctrine.

All dogmas based upon the signification of the words of revelation are liable to be misunderstood. To correct such errors is doubtless a work of great importance, but it belongs to a sphere of investigation entirely distinct from this.

3. A philosophy of Christian Holiness should survey all the facts pertaining to the subject.

The philosophy of any department of knowledge properly denotes—a systematic statement of the phenomena or facts embraced within it; the forces by which they are caused; the methods or laws of their production; and the conditions or principles in accordance with which their production is possible.

These distinctions may be illustrated thus: This pen is now tracing characters upon this page. This tracing is a fact. That which propels the pen is muscular contraction effected by volitional force. The laws of this tracing are the uniform methods which prevail in the art of penmanship. The principles are those conditions of form, embracing straight lines, angles, circles, and curves, by which alone the formation of letters is possible.

So, Christian lives are traced in characters "known and read of all men." Those lives are facts—each made up of myriads of minor facts—every one of which became a fact by the operation of certain forces, and those forces found expression in those facts by the pathways of certain unvarying uniformities called laws, all along which they were hedged in by impassable conditions called principles.

Our work, therefore, is to scan the facts, ascertain the principles, learn the forces, and deduce the laws. The facts referred to are all those effects of the operation of the physical, mental, and spiritual forces in the religious life, which may be apprehended as distinct from the forces producing them.

Facts are the indexes of laws and the exponents of forces. They are out-cropping lodes that indicate the veins which lie beneath the surface. They are projections which reveal the character and dip of underlying strata. If we would map the veins and layers, it must be by carefully comparing the trend and structure of all points to which we have access. So, the facts of holy living are not to be taken in isolation, and speculative theories founded upon them, but are to be viewed as parts of a connected system, to be adequately comprehended only by those who patiently search for the forces and laws concerned in its development and the principles in accordance with which that development proceeds. Here, as in other fields of truth, facts may seem to conflict, forces may appear to range themselves in mutual antagonism, laws may look discordant, and principles may seem crude; but the earnest inquirer will not rest content without pressing toward the light wherein he may behold forces rightly adjusted, laws wisely adapted, principles clearly revealed, and facts explained in harmony with the divine thoughts. But to do this, there must be a careful collation of all the classes of facts bearing upon the subject, lest those omitted should chance to contain some elements of importance to the final elucidation.

4. A philosophy of this subject should exhibit the principles in accordance with which the experience becomes practicable.

Principles, as here understood, are those elemental or constitutional conditions by which only it is possible for the forces to act at all in this direction. Clearly, then, an omission of principles would, to that extent, invalidate the claim of any work to be a philosophy of this subject.

5. The forces involved, as deducible from the facts and principles, should be carefully weighed.

By force is meant, capacity to produce change; that is, any of the modifications or transformations which occur in the transition from a life of sin to a life of faith, and in the progress of that life. Should any force be overlooked, the facts effected by it would to that extent fail to be understood, or, perhaps, be misunderstood. Hence, our survey must embrace not only the forces numerically, but, as far as practicable, in their relative efficiency likewise.

6. The laws of the subject should be enunciated.

The laws are the uniform methods of action of the physical, mental, and spiritual forces in the production of the changes which reveal themselves as facts. Scarcely less important than the knowledge of a force, is the knowledge how that force acts in practical experience. Therefore, the philosophy which fails to comprehend the laws of its subject will, in the same ratio, ever be liable to the charge of inutility.

7. The relation of these laws to the fact of personal responsibility should be shown.

Speculation may revel in the wilds of lawless fancy, but true philosophy always bears the stamp of utility upon its brow. Hence, to explain the laws of Christian life and development is but a part of its work. It would avail but little for the carpenter of a shipwrecked craft to explain to his fellows in misfortune the laws of naval architecture, unless he also taught them how to apply those laws in the construction of a boat from the timbers of the wreck. So, a knowledge of the laws of Christian purity needs to be applied in the matter of personal obligation, in order to reach the high results that are desirable.

CHAPTER II.

THE EXPERIMENTAL FACTS STATED.

Having thus briefly indicated what is *not*, and what *is* included in the present undertaking, we now proceed to consider the facts involved in the subject, as gathered with strict impartiality from all the experiences of which the author has knowledge.

1. PRE-REGENERATE FACTS OF EXPERIENCE.

1. Of these, the first to be noted is *a universal consciousness of guilt*.

The existence of the various religions of the world—both true and false—with their diverse methods of propitiating the favor of the gods, expresses the universal consciousness that guilt is the horrid nightmare whose suffocating burden presses peace and joy from the heart of man. It is this sense of guilt that drives the sinner to his Savior for relief. It is the one engrossing thought which prostrates him as a helpless penitent at the foot of the cross. To his mind, salvation from guilt is equivalent to deliverance from the racking tortures of remorse. True, this sense of guilt is not in all cases equally pungent. When persons have been trained to a life of prayer, and taught frequently to repent of sin, it is not unusual for such to be almost destitute of the painful emotions which characterize the penitence of those less favored—they exhibiting chiefly an earnest longing for the good to be found in religion, or a calm purpose to seek God because it is necessary and right. Yet, this in no wise conflicts with the general fact stated above. On the contrary, the settled, though unemotional, conviction which they have is a confirmation of the fact, inasmuch as it is the stratified deposit from an experience that has been often tossed with emotions of guilt for separate acts of wrong.

2. The second pre-regenerate fact of experience is, *a corruption of the nature*, as universal as the guilt, and anterior to it in time.

This is the fruitful soil from which spring all the guilt-entailing actions of men. We shall consider it under three heads:

(1) *Original* depravity, or the depravity of *loss*. Adam was created with a two-sided nature. The animal—embracing his appetites, propensities, and desires—linked him by means of his senses to the material and the tangible. The spiritual—comprising his reason, conscience, and spiritual affections—united him by means of affinities, truth, and law, to the spiritual and divine. These natures were so adjusted that the spiritual, with

the assistance of God's indwelling Spirit, which was given as the complement of his spiritual affections to fill his consciousness with the bliss of divine communion, was capable of retaining complete supremacy.

But when, in the exercise of his volitional freedom he sinned, the divine life fled out of him; the complement of his better nature was lost; the counterpoise had therefore ceased, and the adjustments were no longer equable. He was depraved; that is, he had lost the proper balance of his nature, in the flight of the divine life by which the equipoise had been maintained. The consequence could not be other than the exhibition of an undue and hitherto unnatural bias toward the objects of sense, and a corresponding indifference to the objects of spiritual affection. The preponderance of inclination changed at once from the lofty aspirations of purity and joy to the groveling propensities of sense and selfishness.

The vacuums in his affections and consciousness, occasioned by the withdrawal of the divine life, stimulated cravings which could only be partially satisfied by a more and more intense self-life which continually swept the tendencies of the nature further and further from their original bearings. But, "as by the offense of one judgment came upon all men to condemnation; even so by the righteousness of one the free gift came upon all men unto justification of life." That is, as the counterbalancing divine life was unconditionally lost to all the race by Adam's sin, so, it was unconditionally restored to all by Christ's intervention; and, therefore, every infant is *in this respect* precisely in the condition that he would have been if Adam had not fallen. By this we mean that every child has freely given to him as his birth-right, under the atonement, such a measure of the indwelling Spirit of God, that, were there no other disabilities pressing upon him, he would be just as favorably pre-inclined to the right as Adam was before his sin. But, unfortunately for humanity, while the indwelling Spirit was restored, the effect of its loss had gone beyond the mere fact of loss and perpetuated itself in—

(2) *Acquired* depravity, or the depravity of *degeneracy*. By the fundamental laws of cause and effect, and of moral affinity, the constitution, thus biased toward sin, would in every subsequent act of guilt crowd the depravation a little further, until a degree of perversion would ensue measured only by the opportunities afforded and the susceptibilities of the nature itself. This species of depravity may be most conveniently considered under three aspects:

A. Physical. The formation of any habit that debilitates or perverts the natural and healthful functions of the bodily organs, is a corresponding depravation of the body. The appetites may be educated to the selection of the most filthy and noxious substances, such as tobacco, opium, arsenic, alcohol, etc., in place of those nutrients which nature has provided; or, to the most abominable practices of lust and uncleanness; but it is always a training in depravity which develops the worst capabilities of the nature.

B. Mental. By the mutual interaction that is perpetually going on between body and mind, physical depravity passes directly into the mental, in the consciousness that reason and manhood are enslaved by the power of domineering appetite. Wherever false views of true manhood prevail; wherever prejudice blinds the mind to truth; or error is maintained for its apparent advantages; or the emotions are deadened to their appropriate excitants, or alive mainly to unnatural stimulants; or the fripperies of fashion are esteemed more than duty, or the blandishments of pleasure more than righteousness; there is mental depravity as degrading as it is destructive.

C. Spiritual. This is found wherever the longings of the spiritual nature are met with anything short of an infinite object, or the conscience is constrained to be aught but supreme, or the final law of action is anything but duty.

Acquired depravity, in either of the above forms, may arise from either of two sources: *a.* It may be voluntarily induced by sin, which is a wrong act or state of the will in reference to some matter of moral obligation, and which is always and necessarily depraving. *b.* It may be impressed by bad educational influences, such as the demoralizing agencies of social life.

(3) *Hereditary* depravity, or the depravity of *congenital perversion.* The laws of descent are as fixed and changeless as those which control the planetary movements. Men rely upon them with unquestioning confidence in the improvement of domesticated animals, and by them effect any desired changes in the individual which the possibilities of the species will permit. The ground of reliance is this: A habit in the parent tends to impress an inborn habit, or constitutional predisposition to the same habit in the progeny. This law is unvarying; the numerous apparent exceptions being only illustrations of neutralizing or overbalancing impressions received, (perhaps from the other parent,) by the operation of the same law.

In estimating its results in any given case, it should always be borne in mind that in every individual two lines of descent from his *parents* are immediately converged, while a single step back, these lines are intermingled with other lines from his grand-parents; and so on backward indefinitely, till we perceive that each person must be the product of an innumerable multitude of modifying forces which it is impossible for us to estimate, and yet which sufficiently account for all the apparent deviations from the established laws of descent. As a curious fact bearing upon this point, we quote from the Report of the Superintendent of the Insurance Department of New York for 1867 : "In considering merely the question of hereditary influences on mortality, the following table will exhibit to the eye the fact that, if we go back only a dozen generations in the direct ancestral line, the blood of 8,190 different persons commingles with that of our own children, and in each one of their ancestors' veins flowed a scarlet current of life equally freighted with infinite ancestral tendencies."

In the descending line, assuming husband and wife to have four children, and that this double or quadruple multiplication will continue for only twelve generations, we see that our own blood will inspire or misguide 5,592,404 different human beings.

Tabular Illustration:

Total,		8,190 ancestors.
12th	"	4,096
11th	"	2,048
10th	"	1,024
9th	"	512
8th	"	256
7th	"	128
6th	"	64
5th	"	32
4th	"	16 great-grandparents.
3rd	"	8 grandparents.
2nd	"	4 parents.
1st generation,		Husband and wife.
2nd	"	4 children.
3rd	"	16 grandchildren.
4th	"	64 great-grandchildren.
5th	"	256
6th	"	1,024
7th	"	4,096
8th	"	16,384
9th	"	65,536
10th	"	262,144
11th	"	1,048,576
12th	"	4,194,304
Total,		5,592,404 descendants.

Every man is what he is, at birth, by the action of fixed laws for which he is not responsible. His responsibility begins only with opportunities of improvement.

We have already said that when Adam sinned he acquired depravation by the act. He may have been penitent and regenerated before his first child was conceived; but regeneration, being a supernatural gift, could not be transmitted, either before the fall or after it.

Hence the laws of descent, fixed in the very constitution of organic life, must have caused Cain to inherit depravity from his parents. To this he added *acquired depravity* in the murder of his brother; and his children must have inherited not only his inherited depravity, but the fearful addition of his acquired depravity. Thus the stream flowed on, widening and deepening and intensifying in every generation, till the whole earth had "corrupted its way before God." Now blend together all the warping and disorganizing influences of acquired and hereditary depravity flowing through the ages, and the wonder is, not that men are as bad as they are, but that they are not a thousand fold worse, as they certainly would be were it not for the antagonizing influences of grace acting through the same laws of descent.*

---

* The law that wrought such havoc, had other possibilities. Though regeneration, because supernatural, could not be transmitted, *yet its elevating and purifying effects on the mind might be,* because they were certain definite impressions upon the constitution which, by that fact, became subject to the laws of descent. One great object that God had in choosing Israel as his peculiar people doubtless was, that the gradual elevation of the people, by the laws of hereditary descent, might build up a national breakwater against the tide of depravity in

3. The third pre-regenerate fact is, *contrition for sin.*

This implies, (1) self-condemnation for the misdeeds of the past, and (2) grief for the sinfulness involved.

Memory recalls the acts and dispositions of life's record, and Conscience sits in judgment pronouncing its condemnation of the wrong. The reason renders its verdict in strict accordance with the conscience; and the spiritual affections, under the stimulus of the Divine Spirit, grieve over the wreck and loss.

Grief fixes the attention, while the law of assosociation hunts out of all the chambers of the soul the dust-covered records of forgotten scenes, only to have them condemned before the same tribunal, and thus the process goes on till it culminates in—

other nations. So, the long-hoped-for millennium of the race, if it ever comes, must come in the inborn virtues of the children, springing from the regenerated hearts and congenitally improved natures of the parents. Regeneration can not be inborn; but an improved susceptibility of conscience may be. Communion with God can not be inherited; but veneration for him, and benevolence toward man, may be. "Between the inborn moral nature of the well-constituted civilized person and the brutal nature of the lowest savage, all question of education and cultivation put aside, the difference as a physical fact is not less than that which often exists between one species of animals and another." (Maudsley's *Physiology and Pathology of Mind,* p. 143.)

4. The fourth pre-regenerate fact, namely, *repentance for sin.*

This differs from contrition, in that it passes from the state of grief into the act of seeking a *remedy*—in the *abandonment of sin.*

Contrition may be long continued—shading years with sadness, and circling only in the same beaten track of sorrow and self-reproach. Repentance has writhed under the lash—has groaned with the grief—and now emerges into the the realm of decisive self-emancipation. It is rebellion against the tyranny of a life-time. It is a cutting loose from the anchorage of years. It is breaking away from associations that have become interlaced with all past experiences. It is abandoning, at sea, the only craft in which he has ever sailed. It is cutting the fabric away from the loom in which it has been woven.

But while it is self-emancipation, it is not spiritual deliverance. While it is rebellion, it is not successful revolution. While it is forsaking one anchorage, it is not grappling another. While it is breaking away from old associations, it is not the formation of regenerating substitutes. While it is abandoning a leaky and sinking craft, it is not walking the deck of a monarch of the deep. While it is cutting the fabric from the loom which has fashioned life so sadly, it is not giving its unwoven threads to a better.

5. The fifth pre-regenerate fact is, *belief in Christ for present salvation.*

This belief is two-fold: (1) It is the intellectual credence given to his word, as a word of undoubted veracity. (2) It is an actual, hearty *reliance* of the soul upon Christ as a *present Savior.*

It is the experience of a patient with his physician in the crisis of a dangerous disease. He affirms most positively his ability to master the disorder, and the patient has perfect confidence in this statement of his skill. But this faith—while it is an important prerequisite to the right use of the means—will never, of itself, prove efficacious.

The doctor prescribes. And now the real heart-faith of the patient is to be tested. If, without reserve or deviation, he throws himself upon the remedies specified, his faith is complete and the result is a cure. But if he reasons—"The doctor certainly *can* cure me, but his medicines are bitter and his regime is painful, and I will try to get well without them"—he only proves the inefficiency of a merely intellectual faith, and his own folly.

In Christian experience, the conviction of the absolute truthfulness of God's word is the immediate antecedent of a complete surrender to the power of his grace, and an actual claiming of his promised in-working.

2. CON-REGENERATE FACTS OF EXPERIENCE.

1. The first con-regenerate fact of experience is, *a mysterious, internal change* or *transformation.* This change includes several things:

(1) An assurance of *pardon*. The long catalogue of transgressions that have stood like a horrid phalanx arrayed against the soul, seems blotted out in a single instant. They may be remembered in intellectual experiences, but their moral significance is gone—washed away in the blood of atonement. Henceforth they are to exist only as reminders of the infinite mercy that has provided a Substitute to bear their penalty. This assurance of pardon comes like a life-boat to the wrecked mariner—like a reprieve to the doomed and almost hopeless criminal.

(2) A consciousness of *freedom from guilt*, that attests the validity of the assurance. The horrid nightmare that has pressed upon the soul is removed. The consciousness that has hitherto seemed charged with the venom of asps, and has seen Peace chased away with scorpion's stings, now sings to the soft lullaby of quietude of spirit. The dread specter that has haunted the soul

through all its guiltiness has disappeared, and in its place smiles the winning form of Innocence.

(3) Then succeeds the *absence of self-condemnation.* The soul's interests have been adjudicated at a higher tribunal than that of Conscience. The verdict of that higher court has set aside the judgments of the lower, in consideration of the special testimony of Faith in Christ. From this there is no appeal. The final decision has been reached in the court of last resort. The prisoner is acquitted.

(4) Consciousness of *love for God and his people.* A new and strange experience ensues. Hitherto God has seemed so far off, so intangible, and withal so *unloving,* (for the feelings of the heart have belied the teaching of the creeds,) and perchance so frowning! Now he is so nigh, so kind, so forgiving! "We love him, because he first loved us." And when once the spiritual affections feel the impulsions of their true life, they reach out in affinity after everything akin to their newly awakened sensibilities. Hence, having love to God, they "love the brethren" also.

(5) Then follows an absolute and grateful *submission to all the will of God.* Submission there has been in penitence, but it has been per force. It has been a yielding to the prescribed terms of a conqueror. It has been paying the price with-

out which the desired benefit could not be secured. But now it is a submission which runs before all terms; a yielding that anticipates demands, and *invites* the test; a glad, grateful, humble acquiescence that joys in debasing self and exalting Christ. And it is as extensive as it is sincere. It revolts at insubordination. It weeps at the very shadow of inconstancy. It hates the thought of treachery. It loathes the mouthings of hypocrisy. To be His—*entirely* His—FOREVER His, is the purpose of the soul, the longing of the affections. A submission more absolute cannot be conceived—more sincere cannot be possible.

(6) A new-born *zeal to do good* is now displayed. Not from considerations of reward, or motives of policy, but from the free, instinctive promptings of a loving heart. It is the out-gushing of welling sympathy—the breaking forth of pent-up good wishes—the consuming ardors of a world-embracing love. It is a feeling kindled by no transient emotion, seeking no momentary indulgence, and subsiding at no command of stolid Indifference; but its flame has caught from the fires of eternal love, its designs stretch through the life-time, and it sinks to quietness only in the anticipated repose of the everlasting rest.

(7) *Hatred of sin* is now evinced. Not the tame repugnance of mere distastefulness, nor the

more positive antipathy of excited resentments; but the deep abhorrence, the shuddering loathing with which purity detests and abominates sin ; a hatred that scorns compromise as treachery, and that is as exclusive as Life is of Death—as Heaven is of Hell!

(8) *"Joy in the Holy Ghost,"* is another element of his experience. Not merely the gladness of deliverance, nor the added serenity of love, nor yet the superadded happiness of doing good ; but the transporting rapture, the blissful felicity, of a soul fired and thrilled and intoned with the ecstatic exultation of a heaven-born joy!

2. The second con-regenerate fact of experience is, *an outward change corresponding with the inward*—a change differing in prominence and intensity according to the degree of emotions experienced.

These emotions vary, from the calm that succeeds the slightest troubled expression, on through the joy that beams where sadness lately sat, to that supernatural radiance that sometimes almost transfigures humanity as it emerges from the dark realm of broken-hearted penitence into the cloudless sunlight of God's ineffable Love— from the unuttered thoughts of gratitude that follow the receding convictions of the heart, on through the whispered breathings of joy that chase away the sighs of contrition, to the bursting gladness of the soul as unbidden hallelujahs break where only sobs were heard. The outward changes indicate the reality, while they cannot measure the extent of the inward work.

3. POST-REGENERATE FACTS OF EXPERIENCE.

1. A period of *joyful triumph* usually comes.

One victory has been gained, so new, so strange, and with such a consciousness of added power, that it seems as though Life's grand conquest had been achieved. This is rather a feeling than a conclusion. It may be a seeming rather than a belief; but it is the Soul's reveling in its new-found joy. The duration of this period may be greater or less—dependent, perhaps, upon causes which we know not how to estimate—but sooner or later it is succeeded by—

2. A sad discovery of *indwelling sin*.

This discovery is usually made in the direction of previous indulgences, or of constitutional predispositions, or of both combined. Example: Suppose a convert has been greatly addicted to the use of intoxicating drinks, and has a constitutional tendency to fretfulness and anger. He may feel no desire for his accustomed stimulants for a time, but sooner or later the appetite usually revives, and often seems the more rampant from its rest. Here, then, is an unlooked-for conflict;

and as it rages, his constitutional tendency feels the excitement, and fretfulness and perhaps anger supervene.

3. Then arise *consternation and confusion.*

With his discovery of this state of things comes a feeling of consternation which it is difficult to describe. He is not merely surprised—he is alarmed and horrified. The regeneration in which he has joyed so much seems vitiated and belied. He has been conscious of placing himself unreservedly in the hands of his Savior, to be fashioned as He would. He has felt the regenerating power of divine grace, and *knows* that a mighty change was accomplished within.

But now the fair fabric of his hopes is all in ruins. The heart that he has not ceased to offer as a "living sacrifice," is polluted. The faith that he thought had emancipated him, lies quivering beneath the onslaught of his old masters. The blood that he supposed had saved, after all his effort and all his joy, has not saved.

He is overwhelmed with confusion. He knows not what to think. What struggle can be successful, if this has not been? What hope can he find in the midst of such defeat? He sinks for a moment in stupor, paralysis, and inaction. The burden of his disappointment presses him to the earth. He is amazed—confounded—overwhelmed.

His disaster seems irreparable; his loss, insufferable.

But he has learned to pray; and now something draws him to the Mercy-seat. He falls before it in deep abasement. His pleadings are sobs. His eloquence is helplessness. His faith is the refuge of despair. But anon a soothing consciousness of an unseen Presence re-inspirits him, and he is found—

4. *Rallying to the struggle.*

But it is the gathering energy of desperation. It is the blindfold advance in the teeth of the storm. It is the groping after a path in the darkness. And yet it has its mitigations and encouragements. There is an ever-present consciousness that *he did not mean* to raise the vile spirit that taunts him. And there is likewise a clear recollection that *he did mean* to be all God wanted him to be. Putting the consciousness and recollection together, he says: "It is not all my fault; and though I cannot understand why God did not take all this away when I lay passive in his hands, yet he did much for me and will help me now."

5. Then *alternate victories and defeats* supervene.

In his onward progress, victories and defeats alternately cheer and depress him. Sometimes he finds periods of conquest and joy, when he stands upon the mountain-top and exults in God his Savior. Then occurs an interval of doubts and sadness, in which he seems to have lost all that he had previously gained. Thus his life is checkered over with the "ups and downs" of changing feeling.

But, in the midst of all his discouragements, a careful analysis of experience will disclose the fact that there have been substantial gains. Weak points have been permanently strengthened. Some besetting infirmities have been disciplined away. Here and there a root-sin of the nature has been eradicated, or so deadened that its once frequent sprouting annoys but little.

Yet there are points of character that have proved invulnerable. Prayers and efforts have been dashed against them in vain. As they lift their proud fronts in the foreground of introspective vision, their very presence mocks his hopes.

But now he is told that the "blood of Jesus *cleanseth from all unrighteousness;*" and the blessed truth sinks down and down till it stands in the immediate presence of the *deepest want of his nature.* Its presence is inspiration. Its softest assurances are electric thrills. Its calmly firm commands are trumpet-calls. The soul girds itself for another conflict, with victory in its eye.

6. *Then comes the cleansing.*

The work is begun by complete divestiture. The consecration of penitence is renewed with a deeper significance. The pledges of fidelity are re-uttered with a fuller meaning.

> "Thy sovereign right, thy gracious claim
>   To every thought and every power,
>   Our lives, to glorify thy name,
>   We yield in this accepted hour.

> "Fill every chamber of the soul;
>   Fill all our thoughts, our passions fill;
>   Till, under thy supreme control,
>   Submissive rests our cheerful will."

Such the pledge and such the prayer! Then, when the sacrifice is complete, Faith lays hold upon the Sanctifier, and cries:

> "'Tis done! Thou dost this moment come;
>   My longing soul is all thine own;
>   My heart is thy abiding home;
>   Henceforth I live for thee alone.

> "The altar sanctifies the gift—
>   The blood insures the boon divine;
>   My outstretched hands to heaven I lift,
>   And claim the Father's promise mine."

In the light and joy of this new experience our convert lives an exulting life. His old inward foes are dead, and in triumph he sings:

> "When God is mine, and I am his,
>   Of paradise possessed,
>   I taste unutterable bliss,
>   And everlasting rest."

7. *The re-awakenings.*

Strange that a work so sincerely wrought, and apparently so deep and thorough, should prove still defective! Yet, the experience of multitudes shows that what they were taught, and really supposed, to be the complete cleansing of their natures, still needs a supplementary work.

Sooner or later his rest is disturbed; not by the old besetments, for grace has conquered them. But the removal of these from the sphere of attention has allowed others, whose existence was perhaps unsuspected, to come into view; and now he finds that his cleansing was only measured by his light and knowledge, and that as other things are revealed he needs a repetition of the process.

8. *The renewed cleansings.*

Again the process is repeated. And thus on through life, as fast as unholy tendencies are revealed, he applies to the sanctifying blood and feels its efficacy, till at last he sinks to rest—a holy man, sleeping in Jesus—because his precious blood has cleansed, not once nor twice, but *every time* that a new discovery of depravity prompted the prayer for aid.

[Up to this point the word soul has been used as synonymous with spirit.]

CHAPTER III.

THE FORCES ENGAGED.

In seeking for the forces engaged in the work of Christian maturity, we may pass by, as not specially relevant, the pre-regenerate facts before stated, and come at once to the con-regenerate and post-regenerate facts as exhibiting the legitimate field for the operation of these forces, as "capacities to produce change."

The first con-regenerate fact has been stated to be, "A mysterious internal change or transformation," page 18, including—

"Assurance of pardon;"
"Consciousness of freedom from guilt;"
"Absence of self-condemnation;"
"Consciousness of love for God and his people;"
"Absolute and grateful submission to God's will;"
"A new-born zeal to do good;"
"Hatred of sin;" and
"Joy in the Holy Ghost."

The second con-regenerate fact is, "An outward change corresponding with the inward." Here we find man's spirit-faculties engaged in harmony with the energy of the Holy Spirit, and securing some degree of co-operation of his psychical (soul) and physical powers. The forces thus far discovered, then, are *spirit, psychic,* and *physical.*

But let us survey the post-regenerate facts, and see if they disclose any additional forces. Those facts have been given, in pages 22–27, as

" A period of joyful triumph ;"
" A sad discovery of indwelling sin ;"
" Consternation and confusion ;"
" Rallying to the struggle ;"
" Alternate victories and defeats ;"
" The cleansing ;"
" The re-awakening ;" and
" The renewed cleansing."

A careful examination of these facts fails to discover any new force, inasmuch as the indwelling sin referred to is only a wrong state or condition of some parts of man's nature. Before considering these forces in detail, it will be necessary to discriminate between the different parts of man's nature, as spirit, soul, and body.

The human spirit is that intelligent, self-conscious, free and non-material manifestation of the divine power, which is individualized by the conditions of soul-development under the laws of human propagation, and which is known to itself in its own consciousness, and is capable of thinking that matter cannot think. It comprehends:—

Intelligence, including perception of facts and relations, and intuitions of truth; character-affinities, including (originally) affectional communion with God; intuitions of futurity; desires and emotions; the reversional faculty; the ideational faculty; habit-constitution; moral free-will; consciousness; conscience; and instincts.

The human soul is the animal soul ennobled to be the complement of the human spirit, and constituted the spirit's medium of communication with the external world through the body. It comprehends:—Inferior intelligence, embracing sense-perceptions and adaptive reason; desires and emotions; habit-susceptibility; imagination; affections; instincts; memory; and will.

The *difference*, therefore, is this:

First, that which they seem to possess in common is *of a much higher order* in the spirit than in the soul.—E. g.—(1) Each has intelligence; but, while the soul's intelligence is only that of sense-perception, and adaptive reason, that of the spirit embraces perception of facts and relations and intuitions of truth. (2) Both have affections; but, while those of the soul are merely personal, those of the spirit rise to the moral grandeur of character-affinities, and communion with God. (3) Both have desires and emotions; but those of the soul relate only to its instincts, while those of the spirit soar to the altitude of its spiritual capacities, and thrill its consciousness and conscience through. (4) Both have memory; but that of the soul treasures only facts of sense-experience, while that of the spirit reverts to and recalls all the past of which it has knowledge— as well its truths and relations, as its facts. (5) Both have imagination; but, while that of the soul is little more than false or whimsical perceptions, that of the spirit is endowed with all the ideationally creative powers of poesy and art. (6). Both have will; but, while that of the soul is restricted to a choice of means to a desired end, that of the spirit is alternative in reference to right and wrong, good and evil, the true and the false. (7) Both have instincts; but, while that of the soul has respect only to self-existence, self-enjoyment, and the propagation of the species, that of the spirit comprehends the lofty possibilities of the consciously moral and possibly immortal. (8) Both have habits; but, while those of the soul pertain only to the physical and sense-life, those of the spirit develop the grandest possibilities of spiritual communion and immortal destiny.

Second, the spirit has three endowments which have no copy, however feeble, in the soul, viz., *intuitions of futurity, consciousness,* and *conscience*.

True, some might suppose, on first thought, that the winter food-provisions of some animals, and the nest and house-building propensities of some birds and animals, indicate an instinct of futurity in them, which, if existing, certainly proves a possibility of the same in the human soul. Also, that the shame which dogs and elephants seem to feel when rebuked, indicates a kind of conscience, while their apparently cherished resentments and measured revenge proclaim a consciousness of having been wronged.

In reply, it may be urged that animals have no apprehension of coming wants, but simply obey a present impulse in those acts that seem to be thus on-looking. As to the shame referred to, its external developments are not at all unlike simple fear in the same animals; hence, it is to be regarded as no more than fear. That the resentments and revenge are purely instinctive, appears from the fact that they will arise just as soon, upon occasion, when the animal is itself encroaching upon the rights of others, as when acting simply upon the defensive. Hence we conclude that those three endowments are the regal qualities of spirit, especially differentiating it from soul.

The human body is the material frame exhibiting the organizing power of the soul-life in the functions of absorption, assimilation, circulation, nutrition, excretion, reproduction, respiration or calorification, motion, habit-evolution, and spirit-unfoldment.

In these we find the three classes of forces already named:

1. *Spirit-forces.*

These embrace such energies of the Divine Nature as are concerned in human redemption; and likewise the energies of the particular human spirit, which is passing through the several changes already denoted as facts of experience. They also embrace those energies employed by Satan to hinder the work.

2. *Psychical forces.*

These include all the *soul*-forces involved in these facts.

3. *Physical forces.*

The physical forces employed are all those powers of the body which, as instruments of the soul and spirit, are with greater or less success used in the prosecution of the grand aim of life; and likewise those perverted energies (if such there be) which cannot be constrained into the service of Holiness. These powers may be classified thus:

1. Vital force—maintaining the ordinary in-

voluntary processes of life, viz., respiration, circulation, nutrition, growth, periodicity, etc.

2. Sensibility-co-operating force—operating through sensitive nerve-vitality.

3. Automatic, or reflex-activity force—acting immediately, upon occasion, without awaiting the intervention of any mental process, as in involuntary starts from falling, winking, dropping hot bodies, etc., which are often accomplished before thought has time to begin, and therefore before judgment can decide or will command.

Just here we are met by a fact of fundamental importance, namely: There is a law of activity, down deep amid the foundation principles of being, deeper than depravity, deeper than purity, *below all moral distinctions*, which may be stated thus: *Any mental action, voluntarily repeated, induces a spontaneous tendency to its continued repetition.* It is the law of spirit-*habit*. Complemental to this law of spirit-activity is a psychical susceptibility, and also a structural adaptability of brain and nerves, furnishing the physical *conditions* for the development of habit, which is, in general terms, only a *customary mode of action* by the operation of this law and its corresponding psychical and structural susceptibility.

The importance of this fact in common life can scarcely be overestimated, because it is by it that the marvelous acquisitions of skill in the arts, etc., are possible, as well as by it that men become addicted to and confirmed in those practices of good or evil which, to a great extent, make reputation and give permanence to character.

Physiologically speaking, as will more clearly appear further on, HABIT may be defined as a *secondary automatic movement* or *reflex action of a nervous center and its efferent nerves*. And whether it be induced by an anatomical change of the tissue, or whether its *modus operandi* must remain a profound secret, the fact is the same—there is a secondary automatic movement *established*, which is in direct physical correspondence with the *psychic* as well as *psychologoical* law, namely: *Any mental action voluntarily repeated induces a spontaneous tendency to its continued repetition;* and the three combined in an established mode of action constitute a habit of the life. "Habit constitutes a true return to automatism, and it is never perfect unless when it is entirely unconscious." (*Ribot, Heredity*, p. 227.)

4. Will-co-operating force—largely muscular contractile energy, manifested through motor nerve-vitality.

5. Mind-conditionating force—a physical status determining or precluding certain mental manifestations, as when the brain is narcotized or

stimulated by certain drugs into the state referred to.

In order to a proper understanding of this part of the subject, it will be necessary to give some details of structure, and dwell at considerable length upon the various functions of the brain and nervous system. But before doing this, we wish most emphatically to disclaim all sympathy with the materialistic speculations to which the science of physiology has given rise, and at the same time to enter a most positive demurrer to the dogmatic conservatism that trembles in terror at every approach of the glass of the microscopist or knife of the anatomist. Let Science speak, and let her voice be heard, whether her interpreter be Jew or Gentile, Believer or Atheist; only let us be sure to separate her facts and deductions from the assumptions and non-authorized deductions of speculatists, of whatever school of thought.

The nervous system of man is divided into two great branches, distinguished by their respective functions. That portion which presides over the locomotory, respiratory, sensitive, and intellectual functions, is called the cerebro-spinal system; while that which controls the functions of the vegetative life, *i. e.*, absorption, assimilation, circulation, nutrition, excretion, and reproduction, is designated as the ganglionic, or great sympathetic system, the object of which seems to be, to associate the different parts of the body in such a manner that stimulus applied to one organ may excite the activity of another, and that by a function which is neither physical nor chemical, but vital.

In the composition of the nervous system are two kinds of tissues, distinguished from each other by their color, structure, and mode of action:

(1) White substance or fibrous tissue, ultimate nervous filaments or threads averaging about a ten-thousandth of an inch in diameter in the brain and spinal cord, and about a two-thousandth of an inch in the nerves.

(2) Gray substance, called also cineritious matter or vesicular neurine, found in the center of the spinal cord, at the base of the brain in isolated masses, as a continuous layer on the surface of the upper and middle brain, (cerebrum and cerebellum,) and in the ganglia of the great sympathetic. This substance consists of vesicles or cells from a four-thousandth to a three-hundredth of an inch in diameter, of various forms and sizes, imbedded in a grayish, granular, intercellular substance, (frequently containing granules of grayish coloring matter,) intermingled with

nervous filaments originating from, or terminating in, the nerve-cells. Every *collection* of such gray matter is called a *ganglion* or *nervous center*, the special function of which is to receive impressions conveyed to it by the nervous filaments, and send out through them answering impulses to be transmitted to distant organs. A bundle of nervous filaments enveloped in a sheath of tough tissue—similar in constitution to that of sinews and ligaments—looks like fibers of spun glass, and is called a nerve.

In structure, these filaments possess the following properties:

A. A colorless, transparent, tubular membrane, in the cavity of which is lodged—

B. A semi-fluid, tubular marrow, which coagulates soon after death, and presents a peculiar glistening aspect, and is known as the *"white substance of Schwann."* This contains in its cavity—

C. A narrow, ribbon-shaped cord, firm, semi-transparent, of a grayish color, known as the *axis-cylinder*, and is the only *active element* of the nerve. Its use is simply as an organ of transmission. The *direction* of the transmission has been taken as the ground of distinction between the two classes of nerves. When one is distributed upon an expanded surface and is capable of transmitting *inwardly* to the nervous center any impression induced by the application of any physical stimulus to that surface, it is called a nerve of sensation, or sensitive or afferent nerve. When a nerve is distributed among muscular fibers and is capable of causing muscular contraction by carrying the impulse outward from the nervous center, it is called an excitor, or motor, or efferent nerve. And the *impulse* thus returned by the ganglion or center, in answer to a stimulus or impression sent to it, is called its *reaction* or *reflex action*. Bundles of nervous filaments connecting different ganglia are called *commissures*.

Thus the entire nervous system is made up of ganglia, commissures, and nerves—the two latter identical in anatomical character. The office of nervous filaments is to conduct an influence along their axis longitudinally, either from periphery (outside) to center, as in the case of nerves of the senses, or from center to periphery, as in the case of nerves which convey the mandates of the will to the muscles. In this office of conduction the whole extent of nerve-fiber is the seat of an active molecular change.

Confining our attention now to the cerebrospinal system, we find it to consist of the following parts, namely:

A. The *spinal cord*—lodged within the canal

of the back-bone, and extending from the base of the skull to about the origin of the lowest rib.

B. The *medulla oblongata*—apparently a continuation of the spinal cord within the head.

C. The *sensory ganglia*—several masses of nerve-substance arranged in pairs along the floor of the skull.

D. The *cerebellum,* or little brain—situated above and behind the medulla.

E. The *cerebrum,* or great brain—two large convoluted lobes superimposed above all the others, and called *hemispheres.*

These five centers of nervous substance known as *ganglia,* each with its distinct function, are bound together into one system. The nervous appliances by which each center is able to discharge its functions are, in order, as follows:

a. From the spinal cord are given off thirty-one pairs of nerves—each arising by two roots from the cord itself—which combine upon leaving the spinal column, and are distributed to the muscles and skin of the body and limbs, serving the functions of motion and sensation, including the special sense of touch. The posterior of the two roots serves the purpose of sensation, and the anterior of motion; but when combined into one nerve-cord, it possesses both of these characteristics.

The functions of the spinal cord are three-fold: (a) That of a nerve-center, *i. e.*, a power of receiving impressions conveyed to it as a stimulus from without, and reflecting them immediately through the motor nerves without the judgment or co-operation of the brain, causing adaptive movements independently of consciousness or volition, by a process *purely physical*. This is proved by the fact that in cases of division of the cord below the point where the respiratory nerves are given off, both voluntary motion and sensation cease; yet a slight touch of the foot will cause it to be drawn up, although the man himself is unconscious of the act. So a decapitated frog will, with one of its feet, displace an irritating agent applied to its body; and a centipede, with a section of the spinal cord removed from the middle of the trunk, and the hinder legs consequently completely paralyzed, will continue to move them, often forcing itself in directions in which it does not desire to go, as indicated by the opposing movements of the fore legs which are still under control of the will. In a state of health, the reactions of the spinal cord are often so sudden that the movements are executed before we feel any painful sensation, or even fairly comprehend why they take place, as in impulsive withdrawal of the hand from a heated body; also the involuntary throwing of the limbs into a position to break a sudden fall. (*Dalton's Human Physiology*.)

Concerning these well established facts, Mr. Maudsley (*Physiology and Pathology of Mind*, p. 67) thus reasons: "The spinal cord has, so to speak, its memory; the reaction which it displays, in consequence of a particular impression conveyed to it from without, does not vanish issueless, leaving the ganglionic cells unmodified after its force has been expended. With the display of energy there is a coincident change or waste of nervous elements; . . . and the nutritive repair, replacing the loss which has been made, must plainly take the form or pattern created by the energy and coincident material change. Thereby the definite activity is to some extent realized or *embodied* in the *structure* of the *spinal cord*, existing there for the future as a motor residuum, or as, so to speak, a potential or abstract movement; and accordingly there is a tendency to the recurrence of the particular activity—a tendency which becomes stronger with every repetition of it, . . . until at last they [the particular activities or movements] are firmly fixed in the constitution of the cord, become a *part* of the *faculty* of it, and may be accomplished without effort or even without consciousness;—they are the secondary or acquired automatic acts, as described by Hartly."

And Hartly, in his "Theory of the Human Mind," very sensibly declares that the acts just alluded to "are rather to be ascribed to the body than the mind," because they are the results of these functions of nerve-vesicles—the active element of nerve-centers.

There seems to be a triple object of this arrangement: ((a)) To permit the escape of an influence entering by a nerve-filament, into a a number of diverging tracks. ((b)) To combine such entering influences into a new result. ((c)) By permitting lateral diffusion, to take off and keep in store, for a certain duration, a part of the passing influences, thus retaining a residuum of the impressions and entitling these centers to the name of registering ganglia. This susceptibility is the great fact by which Habit becomes possible.

"In the different ganglionic centers is a specific power of reaction to certain impressions made upon organs specially adapted to receive them; the waste following activity is restored by nutrition, and a trace or residuum remains embodied in the constitution of the nervous center, becoming more complete and distinct with each succeeding repetition of the impression; an acquired nature is grafted on the original nature of the cell by virtue of its plastic power." (*Maudsley, P. and P. of Mind*, p. 91.)

(*b*) The second function of the spinal cord is that of an intermuntiant nerve, *i. e.*, a nerve of communication through its commissures between its own nerves and the *higher* nervous centers, by which it passes on the effect of the outward stimulus to the higher centers, and in return receives orders from them to be transmitted to the efferent or outward discharging nerves. It is by this function that the brain receives the impressions made upon the skin, (that may have been already responded to by a reaction of the cord causing some muscular movements,) and recognizes them in consciousness, and perhaps superadds some voluntary actions.

(*c*) The third function of the spinal cord is to furnish a pathway for certain nervous channels of sensation between the cerebral sensorium, *i. e.*, the cerebral centers, and the nerves of sensation and motion leading to different portions of the body.

The medulla is an extension of the spinal cord, about 1¼ inches long, within the head. Its function is to control respiration by a reflex action occasioned by the stimulus of carbonic acid in the pulmonary vessels and air cells. It also governs deglutition, simple exclamation, sneezing, coughing and yawning, and by means of the auditory and gustatory nerves springing from it controls the senses of hearing and taste, and "also presides over those muscular contractions which constitute the play of the physiognomy." (*Ribot.*)

Passing upward and forward from the medulla, we find a glanglion called *tuber annulare*—sometimes called the "fourth pair"—and the *sensorium commune*, the function of which is to catch the impressions conveyed inward through the nerves, and convert them into *conscious sensations*, the reflex action from which takes the form of *voluntary impulses* designed to stimulate the muscles to contraction. (*Dalton's Physiology*, p. 423.)

"The natural course of a stimulus, all the force of which is not reflected upon an efferent nerve in the spinal centers, is upwards to the sensorium commune, where it becomes the occasion of a new order of phenomena; and, as Pfluger has shown, the law of extension of reflex action, excited by a spinal nerve, observably is from below upwards to the medulla. Having arrived at the ganglionic cells of the sensorium commune, the stimulus may be at once reflected on a motor nerve, for which there is provision in a direct physical path, and *involuntary movements*—sensori-motor—may thus take place in *answer* to a *sensation*, just as involuntary movements take place from the spinal centers *without* any sensation." (*Maudsley, Physiology and Pathology of Mind*, p. 89.) So, this sensori-motor reaction may be excited by "sensation from *within the body*—by the organic stimuli"—as well as by sensations from without. "When the influence of the higher nervous centers" (*i. e.*, the hemispheres) "is weakened by disease, or when an organic stimulus has an abnormal activity, as often happens in insanity, we sometimes see the instinct for food or the sexual instinct manifested with an utter shamelessness. . . . The great revolution effected in the mental nature of man at the time when the organs of reproduction come into functional activity, affords a striking illustration of a physiological effect which in less degree is common to all the organic stimuli." (*Ibid*, p. 95.) The sensori-motor reaction may be excited likewise by "*a stimulus descending from above*. An idea, or an impulse of the will, coming from the higher nervous centers" (*i. e.*, the hemispheres,) "may act upon the ganglionic secondary centers" (as e. g., the sensorium commune,) "and call forth those movements which are commonly reflex to impressions from without." (*Ibid*, p. 97.) An example of this would be, dreams of frightful objects producing starts and screams, as if such objects were really in sight.

Passing upward again we reach four little bodies, the *tubercula quadrigemina,* or *optic ganglia,* giving origin to the optic nerve, and presiding over the sense of sight. By their reflex action the quantity of light admitted to the eye is regulated (by its expansion and contraction) to suit the sensibility of the retina. Continuing upward and forward once more, we come to the *optic thalami,* possessing a peculiar crossed action upon the voluntary movements, and beyond this but little understood. Directly in front of the optic thalami are the *corpora striata*—like that, in functions but little known, but supposed to have some connection with sensation and volition. Far in front of the corpora striata lies the olfactory ganglion presiding over the sense of smell.

Dr. Carpenter has shown the very great probability that the sensory ganglia are a *sensorium commune* through which the mind becomes conscious of all its *states* as well as of its sensations; and that, as the conditions of sensational consciousness are, 1st, an impression on the peripheral (outward) expansion of a sensitive nerve, 2nd, the transmission of nervous force along the nerve, and 3d, an organic change in the sensorium; so, the consciousness of other mental states requires, 1st, an impression on the expanded sheet of gray matter in the convolutions of the hemispheres at the peripheral ends of the nerve-fibers which radiate from the sensory ganglia, 2nd, the transmission of nervous force from this gray matter, as the instrument of the mental faculties, to the sensory ganglia, and 3d, an organic change in the latter as the immediate antecedent of consciousness.

The sensory ganglia are therefore—

1st, Seats of sensational consciousness.

2nd, Seats of the consciousness of all our mental states.

3d, Centers of sensori-reflex movements.

4th, They supply the nervous force which bears the mandates of the will to the muscles of the body; since it has been proved by Sir Charles Bell and C. Bernard that no voluntary movement can be performed without their intervening action.

Directly in the rear of the "fourth pair" is the *cerebellum,* highly convoluted and containing a large amount of gray matter. Its function is to co-ordinate voluntary movements. As all muscular movements are effected by several muscles acting in harmony, and the number and complication of these associated actions are very great in man, some organ must preside over and co-ordinate these actions. Hence this function is assigned to the most important ganglion in the brain, save one.

Roofing all the others, and constituting about nine-tenths of the brain, are the hemispheres or cerebrum, the highest of the nervous centers, consisting of a layer three-sixteenths of an inch thick, of gray substance, of great superficial extent, and thrown into irregular folds or convolutions. Its function is to act as the organ of the intellectual and moral faculties. This is proved by several classes of facts. E. g. In fishes, reptiles, birds, and quadrupeds, the size of the hemispheres is an exact index of their *teachable* intelligence. On removing the hemisphere of a pigeon, association of ideas, perception of the relation of external objects, and memory are destroyed; while sight, hearing, sensibility, and will remain. Intelligence, memory, and judgment are also destroyed in man, in apoplexy and softening of the brain; while other functions not intellectual may still remain. (*Dalton's Physiology*, p. 407.)

The hemispheres are therefore the material instruments through which the immaterial spirit operates. Just as visual consciousness requires that an impression be made upon the retina, and then be transmitted to the sensorium and effect molecular changes therein; so the consciousness of ideas requires that the immaterial spirit make an impression upon the peripheries of the nerves leading to the sensorium commune, that this impression be transmitted, and that the molecular change ensue therein. In both cases the impressing agent is extraneous to the nervous instrument; but in the first it is physical, and in the second it is spirit.

The hemispheres, too, have their reflex action, in which ideas are followed by appropriate actions, provided, the will be in abeyance. The will or executive function of the spirit seems to stand to the hemispheres in the place of a higher nervous center. This reflex action is especially apparent when the power of the will over the current of thought is suspended, *without the loss of power of voluntary motion*, as in persons who are "hypnotized," *i. e.*, in a mesmeric sleep.

"The cortical [external, rind-like] cells of the hemispheres, like the ganglionic cells of the sensory centers and of the spinal cord, may certainly act as nervous centers of independent reaction. Without any volition, or even in direct defiance of volitional effort, an idea which has become active may pass outwards, and produce movements, or some other effect upon the body. The suddenly excited idea of the ludicrous, for example, causes involuntary laughter; the idea of an insult, a quick movement of retaliation; the idea of a beautiful woman, a glow of amatorial passion; the idea of a great impending danger, or of a sudden terrible affliction, serious or even fatal disturbance of the organic life; the idea of an object, sometimes an actual hallucination." (*Maudsley, P. and P. of Mind*, p. 108.) The direction which these reactions may take are downwards upon the motor centers, causing muscular movements either voluntary or involuntary; downwards upon the sensory ganglia, producing sensations as of nausea at the thought of some sickening taste; downwards upon the functions of nutrition and secretion, as the idea of food causing a flow of saliva; a sympathetic idea, a flow of tears; ("and the idea that a structural defect will certainly be removed by a particular act does sometimes so affect the organic action of the part as to produce a cure." *Ibid*, p. 116;) or, they may pass from cell to cell of the cortical centers (of the hemispheres) and be manifested in reflection, and "as the final result of reflection, there may still be a reaction downwards, and consequent outward activity. When that takes place it is *volitional* activity." (*Ibid*, p. 125.)

"In so far as an idea is attended with some feeling, whether of pleasure or of pain, or of a more special character, it is to that extent emotional; and if the feeling preponderate, the idea is obscured, and the state of mind is then called an emotion or a passion." (*Ibid*, p. 129.) As there are two elements which go to the production of an emotion—namely, the organic element and the external stimulus—the character of the emotional result will depend upon the condition of the organic element as well as upon the nature of the stimulus. "The original nature of nerve-element is, however, as nothing in the determination of the special character of the higher emotions, compared with its *acquired* nature as this has been slowly organized in relation to the circumstances of life." (*Ibid*, p. 136.)

"As we justly speak of the *tone* of the spinal cord, by the variations of which its reactions are so much affected, so we may fairly also speak of a *psychical tone*, the tone of the supreme nervous centers, [*i. e.*, the hemispheres] the variations of which so greatly affect the character of the mental states that supervene. And as it appeared when treating of the spinal cord that, apart from its original nature and accidental causes of disturbance, the tone of it was determined by the totality of impressions made upon it, and of motor reactions thereto, which had been organized in its constitution as faculties; so with regard to the supreme centers of our mental life, from the residua of past thoughts, feelings, and actions, which have been organized as mental faculties, there results a certain psychical tone in each individual." (*Ibid*, p. 137.) "The residua of volitions, like the residua of sensations or ideas, remain in the mind and render future volitions of a like kind more easy and more definite." ... "Conscious acquisition becomes unconscious power; and by an organic assimilation of some kind, the will even becomes in certain relations automatic." (*Ibid*, p. 157.)

The foregoing statements are sufficiently explicit in regard to all the forms of physical force before enumerated, except that which has been denominated mind-conditionating force. When we remember that mentality is dependent upon the adequate supply of pure blood to the brain, and that changes in the chemical constituents of the blood either exalt, enfeeble, or suspend mental action—an excess of oxygen intensifying it, a deficiency of phosphorus or oxygen depressing it, and the pressure in large quantities of alcohol, opium, or carbon, holding in abeyance or utterly destroying it—we cannot question the reality of such a thought-modifying physical state as practically amounts to a mind-conditionating force, not as a unit, but as producing the effects that a unit of energy might, viz., modification of mental action.

To such an extent have experiments in this direction been carried, that an eminent physician claimed to be able to produce particular classes of mental states in his patients simply by administering certain drugs.

CHAPTER IV.

THE PRINCIPLES CONCERNED.

Recalling just here the definition of Principles as given on page 4 and illustrated on page 2, as those elemental or constitutional conditions by which only it is possible for the spiritual, psychical, and physical forces to act at all in the direction of salvation, we proceed to inquire: What Principles furnish the conditions for the action of the foregoing forces? The answer evidently is—

1. *Those which relate to God.*

Elemental or constitutional conditions are none other than the nature itself imposes when that nature is absolute; therefore, in seeking for the conditionating elements in question, we must find them in the attributes of the Divine Nature. These attributes necessitate that whatever God does, shall be marked by Goodness, Righteousness, Holiness, and Benevolence. Hence these qualities must stand hedging about all his acts in human Redemption, and constitute just so many impassable barriers defining the channels of his possible activity.

One of the most obvious principles growing out

of the exercise of those qualities is what may be termed—

1. *God's equity in grace.*

"He is not a respecter of persons." Acts 10 : 34. By this is meant that he does not show partiality to any in the matter of personal salvation.

This insures not only that exact and equal justice shall be administered to all according to their actual merit or demerit, but also, that if any personal *free gift* be requisite to the salvation of the individuals of the race, it shall be conferred alike upon all those individuals if it be upon any; because, when all are equally helpless and equally unworthy, to extend the needed aid to some and not to others would be exhibiting a partiality toward the favored ones which could be based upon no *reason*, and therefore would be unjustifiable, inasmuch as Divine Benevolence must regard all with a like pity, and Omniscience could find no special ground of preference. Hence, "The true Light lighteth *every man* that cometh into the world." John 1: 9.

This principle does not inhibit any bestowment of favors of a personal character upon individuals, provided those favors be not of such a nature as that deprivation of them shall bar the salvation of those who are not thus specially honored. E. g. The inspiration of the Prophets was undoubtedly a signal mark of divine approval; but it was not needed by others as a personal gift, in order to enable them to work out their salvation; hence no injustice was done them in not bestowing it upon them as well as upon those who actually received it.

2. Another principle recognizes *different degrees of moral purity as consistent with a Christian character in this life.*

No one acquainted with the interior life of believers can doubt that the same individual may live in communion with God through varying shades of moral purity from regeneration up to the highest attainments of grace. Nor, if human testimony is of any worth, can it be doubted that different persons may stand, relatively to each other, in vastly diverse conditions of spiritual advancement, yet all have the evidence that they please God.

Such being the facts, there must be a principle adjusted to them; and as philosophy requires us to seek the simplest principle consistent with the facts, that is found in the principle here announced, because this is *necessarily implied*, whatever other one may be supposed.

If proof from the Scriptures be needed, we have but to cite the fact that the Thessalonians were regarded by the apostle as already in a very commendable state; for, in his first Epistle to them he credits them with thirteen characteristics as follows: (1) Elected of God, 1: 4. (2) Having "received the word in much affliction," (persecution,) 1: 6. (3) Having received it "with joy of the Holy Ghost," 1: 6. (4) Having become "followers of himself and of God," being "turned from idols to serve the living and true God," 1: 9. (5) Being "in God the Father and in the Lord Jesus Christ," 1: 1. (6) Having a "work of faith and labor of love, and patience of hope in our Lord Jesus Christ," 1: 3. (7) Being "ensamples to all that believe in Macedonia and Achaia," 1: 7. (8) Having "sounded out the word of the Lord not only in Macedonia and Achaia, but also in every place" their "faith to God-ward spread abroad," 1: 8. (9) The word "effectually working" in them, 2: 13. (10) Their brotherly love being shown "toward all the brethren in Macedonia," 4: 10. (11) They being "not in darkness" but "children of the light," 5: 5. (12) Comforting themselves together, and edifying one another, 5: 11. (13) They being Paul's hope, his joy, and his crown of rejoicing, (glorying,) 2: 19.

To *such* Christians Paul wrote: " Now the God of peace himself sanctify you wholly, and may your whole nature, your spirit and soul and body, be preserved blameless when you stand before our Lord Jesus Christ at his appearing. Faithful is He who calls you; He will fulfill my prayer." 1 Thess. 5: 23, 24. (Conybeare and Howson's translation.)

Commendable as their experience was, he here prays for something in advance of it. Their *then* experience certainly was consistent with a Christian character, and the prayed-for advance could not be *less* so; hence, the conclusion is unavoidable, viz.—Different degrees of moral purity are consistent with a Christian character.

3. The third principle is, *the incompatibility of present justification with a present state of moral unfitness for the heavenly world.*

"Who shall lay anything to the charge of God's elect? It is God that justifieth. Who is he that condemneth?" is the triumphant inquiry of the apostle. This was a conclusion from his sublime postulate of faith: "There is now no condemnation to them which are in Christ Jesus, who walk not after the flesh, but after the Spirit. For the law of the Spirit of life in Christ Jesus hath made me free from the law of sin and death." Rom. 8: 1–2.

The word $\delta\iota\kappa\alpha\iota\omega\nu$, *dikaiōn,* here rendered *"justifieth,"* signifies *justification by faith,* as is evident from the apostle's use of it in other places. E. g.

Acts 13: 39. Rom. 2: 13; 3: 20, 24, 26, 28, 30; 4: 2, 3, 5; 5: 1, 9. Gal. 2: 16; 3: 11, 24. It is everywhere regarded as the exact *opposite* of condemnation; so that, to affirm of any one that he is justified in any particular, and, at the same time, is condemned in the same particular, is contradictory and absurd.

But what is meant by justification by faith? To regard and treat one as righteous, by reckoning his faith as righteousness. (See *Robinson's Lexicon* under δικαιόω, *dikaioō*.) Now the question comes: Can spotless righteousness be compatible with a state of unfitness for the home of glorified saints?

Reasoning from the Divine attributes concerned, we see no reason for supposing that any qualification other than those embraced in a character of righteousness can be required. How, then, can that which the God of righteousness has accepted as the *full equivalent* up to that period of such a life of righteousness—viz., the faith which justifies—be less perfectly preparative for heavenly enjoyment than the righteous life itself would be? Surely, it is incumbent upon those who may oppose this view to show some elemental deficiency, or some want of adaptation in the equivalent, as a cause of its assumed inefficiency. Until that is done, we are constrained to regard a state of present justification as tantamount to a state of present fitness for glorification.

Moreover, the objector must meet another difficulty of no less magnitude, viz., the consciousness of the justified spirit of present response to God's claims, up to the highest point of light and ability. Now, to assume that such consciousness may co-exist with a state of unfitness for heaven —should God be pleased *immediately* to make such a transfer—is to confuse all our ideas of fitness in the case, and elevate a mere theological dogma to the detriment if not destruction of all assurance drawn from consciousness and experience.

4. The fourth principle necessarily involved, fixes the grand requisite for admission into heaven:*—"*Be ye holy, for I the Lord your God am holy.*" "According as he hath chosen us in him before the foundation of the world, that we should be holy and without blame before him in love." Eph. 1: 4. "Follow peace with all men and holiness, without which [holiness—see Emphatic Diaglott] no man shall see the Lord." Heb. 12: 14.

---

*For brevity and convenience, we sometimes use the term "heaven" to designate the home of the saints; but we use it only in a general sense, not doubting that the heavenly home of the glorified church will be the "new earth wherein dwelleth righteousness."

Thus we see that the possession of some degree of holiness, and a pressing after larger measures, are required of us *here*, which is precisely what should be expected from the attributes concerned in our salvation. That heaven is a place of holiness, is the common representation of the Bible, as it must be equally the affirmation of Reason, judging from the affinities of the Being whose presence and glory make heaven; hence holiness must be the grand requisite for admission to its sacred enjoyments.

But here the question arises: How much holiness is requisite for admission into heaven? We answer:

(1) Only so much as is involved in the regeneration of the penitent.

(2) Or such additional degree as may be secured by a faithful Christian life.

(3) Or such as it is *supposed* is freely given to dying infants and to every justified spirit in the hour of death.

The last is the belief of many. Yet, when we ask upon what it is based, we find its only foundation to be an inference from two other beliefs, namely: (*a*) That all the good, but only partially sanctified people in the world, cannot be lost. (*b*) Yet without holiness—in greater degree than they possess in life—no one shall see the Lord.

Thence comes the inference: "God must sanctify them in death!"

Now, is it not strange that amid all the promises of God's Word, *not one* distinctly and definitely suggests such a hope, much less the assurance of it? We find therein 292 promises of temporal blessings, 280 relating to troubles, 183 pledging salvation in eternity, 321 relating to the church, and 1219 of spiritual blessings in this life—a grand total of 2295 (counting one verse as a promise)—but not *one* even *hinting* at *death-purification!* If such a death-purgation be the grand reliance of the great mass of believers, why is the door of doubt left so widely ajar here, when so carefully closed elsewhere? Any other matter of solicitude can scarcely be mentioned that has not some promise specially adapted to it; why, then, should this crowning peak of all anxiety be left unarched by a single bow? The *silence* of the Scriptures upon this point is fatally suggestive.

But granting, for a moment, the correctness of this popular view; then it follows that a *free gift* of holiness is made in the hour of death to infants and all believers, not as being necessary to save them from hell—for no justified soul can go there—but to fit them for heaven. And this gift is made WITHOUT THEIR VOLUNTARY CONCURrence, because infants are incapable of it; and if believers, by repentance upon the bed of death, have it, it is wrought in them by supernatural agency, which equals still another free gift to them. But if God can purify a soul in death, without its concurrence, or if he can supernaturally *induce* such concurrence, then he can do the same in life; since it is absurd to suppose that death can have any cleansing, or will-constraining agency. Besides, the attributes already named require in their very nature that *free gifts* of such astounding imports shall be made, if at all, AT THE TIME when they can most effectively serve the design in making them, viz., the glory of God and the good of men.

All God's acts of grace spring from his infinite love. Such love must do the best that it can for the recipient, else it is not infinite love. But according to the opinion under review, that love can and does sanctify men in death as a free gift. Then it can sanctify before death just as well, as a free gift. And by so much as sanctification in life is a better thing than justification, and by so much as it glorifies God and benefits men more, by all this he is bound to give it just as quickly as possible to the justified believer. For, surely, mere justice requires that those who are to be exposed to life's perils, and endure its trials, shall receive as good an outfit as those who escape both. And their security amidst this world's corruptions requires all the purity that God can give them, while his own glory demands that they shall be as good representatives of his purity as free grace can make them, and his infinite love necessitates that his own dear children, whom he regards "as the apple of his eye," shall be furnished with all the protection and aid that his supernatural working and free gifts can bestow; therefore, if God can sanctify the dying Christian by free grace, and the living by the same free grace, and fails to do the latter, he is not only a respecter of persons, in favor of the dying, but is unjust to them in that he has not sanctified them before, and unjust to the living in that he does not sanctify them by free grace at all; because the principles of honor and right demand that a helpless being exposed to such tremendous liabilities shall be guarded in the best possible manner.

For these reasons we are constrained to discard this hypothesis, and fall back upon the first as alone consonant with the principles of the Divine administration, namely: The holiness which is esteemed requisite for heaven is only so much as is involved in the regeneration of the penitent; the additional degree that may be secured by a life of fidelity only *enhancing* the *rewards*, without being the condition of heavenly inheritance. It should, however, be distinctly understood that the experience of added degrees of moral purity, consequent upon fidelity, is the *condition of a life of justification*. That is, one who voluntarily neglects the attainment of such a measure of sanctification as legitimately pertains to and issues from a life of fidelity, must receive pardon for that sin of omission before he can be said to be in a truly justified state here, or be saved hereafter.

Some assume that "God sees in the justified the real conditions of purity," and therefore bestows it, in death, not arbitrarily, but according to the *law* of grace. Then, we ask, why does he not bestow it upon the *living* for the same reason? It surely cannot be because of his consideration of the "shortness of the season" to the dying, as an eminent divine has said, for multitudes of them have lived through many years of Christian experience and had a long season before death; unless he thereby voluntarily condones their lifetime fault, and in effect rewards their spiritual indolence.

It would be well for those who advocate this view to point out *what* "conditions of purity" are to be found in the dying beyond those which exist in the convert, and aside from particular sanctifying faith, which is excluded from this discussion by the fact that the theory which we oppose is framed to account for death-bed sanctifications without the specific action of the subject. If the reader will turn back and read pages 18–21, he will feel the force of this difficulty as he cannot be supposed to do by a mere mental glance at convert-life. In the absence, therefore, of any known "conditions," real or possible, we submit that the hypothesis fails to furnish any satisfactory ground of assurance, and should be abandoned as untenable.

5. Another principle relating to the Divine Being is — *The immediate accomplishment of his part of the work of salvation upon the occurrence of the right conditions in the subject.*

To assume otherwise, is to suppose that a work which God is infinitely desirous to do is held in abeyance, not only when all hindrances have been removed, but likewise without any reason; because, to infer the existence of a retarding reason in him, when there is none in the creature, is to assume an imperfection in him; and if he delays the work without such a reason, he thereby becomes capricious, which is likewise an imperfection. We are thus constrained to admit the imperfection and therefore the undeification of the

Deity, or accept the above as a principle relating to him in the work of human salvation.

6. Still another principle relating to God is — *The necessity of dealing with dissimilar facts in his human subjects as dissimilar, not as similar.*

A distinction was made in the original production, of which this work is an enlargement, between the *me* and the *my*.

The *me* is the totality of essence and attributes comprising this individual being, and concerning which character and actions may be affirmed.

The *my* is anything belonging to the *me* which may be separated from it without its destruction.

Reason asserts the existence in the *me* of a *will-power*, which is such an essential element of the *me* that, were it dissected out, the *me* would not remain.

Consciousness affirms the reality of *volitions*, which are certain contingent results attributable to the will-power, any of which results may be separated from the *me* with no detriment to the complete conception of the *me*. The will-power is a part of the *me*. The volitions are included in the *my*.

The *me* is the *spirit*—embracing intelligence, (including perception of facts and relations, and intuitions of truth;) character-affinities, (including affectional communion with God;) intuitions of futurity; desires and emotions; the reversional faculty; the ideational faculty; habit-constitution; moral free-will; consciousness; conscience, and instincts.

The *my* is the *soul and body*—embracing inferior intelligence, (including sense-perceptions and adaptive reason;) desires and emotions; habit-susceptibility; imaginations; affections; instincts; memory, and will, together with the material frame and all its functions.

Now, if there is no distinction between the *me* and the *my*, every dictionary of every language must have falsely interpreted the discriminations of thought; our fundamental conceptions concerning self-hood as an entity, as distinct from those accidents that may be predicated of it, are all wrong; and the testimony of Reason and Consciousness are misleading. Hence we conclude that the distinction is founded upon a difference in fact.

Every fact has its own peculiar relation to other facts, and no two dissimilar facts can possibly sustain precisely the same relation to others.

It is a fact that God is engaged in the work of human salvation. In relations with this, are the facts in question—the *me* and the *my*. But different and dissimilar as they are, it is impossible that they should stand in the *same* relation to the great fact of Divine interposition for man. Hence arises the necessity that God shall regard, and plan for them according to their dissimilar relations. Nor should it be deemed surprising if the difference in those relations should be found to determine the boundaries of *some* of his acts of grace toward man.

2. *Principles which relate to Man.*

Here, again, the *nature* is the ground from which the principles spring. As we investigate this branch of our subject, it will be well to bear in mind the familiar distinctions between Intellect, Sensibilities, and Will, adding, to complete the statement, the Corporeal Structure. The following propositions will doubtless be accepted, in reference to these several departments of man's being:

First. All mental processes involved in religious experience are subject to the same laws of inter-dependence that obtain in those which relate to other matters not religious. That is, the proper excitant of will is motive; of sensibility, is impression; and of intellect, is fact or truth, in religion, as in other things.

Second. The mere fact that a religious experience has been engrafted into a man's compound nature, will not prevent the physical states from effecting (as casual forces) certain modifications of mental action. E. g. If an overdose of opium will arrest mentality in the unregenerate, a similar dose will no less stupefy the regenerate mind.

From the well known laws involved in mental and physical action as related to religious experience, we deduce the following principles which will need but little amplification, namely :

1. Man must be convicted of *the reality and malignity of his moral disease.*

The proffer of a cure is ever unmeaning in the absence of knowledge of disease. Deliverance from no existing calamity, and salvation from no peril, are sounds without sense. Hence the conviction of helplessness and peril is at the spring of all effort toward relief.

2. He must be convinced that there is *an effectual remedy for him.*

The fact that so few of those who are convinced of the reality can be induced to avail themselves of its benefits, shows how necessary is this assurance. Besides, the laws of mind require, as a condition precedent to earnest and long continued spiritual endeavors, an unshaken faith in their validity, which faith can only be grounded upon an assurance of their adaptation to our state of need ; or, in other words, as the right things to do to secure a relief somewhere provided.

3. He must earnestly desire and determine *to procure its application to himself.*

No sick man is ever healed simply by his knowledge of his disease, or assurance of the existence of a remedy. He must superadd to these a desire to be cured strong enough to induce him to make effort, and a special determination that shall direct the effort in the proper channels.

4. He must be conscious of *the validity of his efforts* to subject himself to the potency of the remedy sought.

Mistakes in this direction might be fatal. Assurance must *be* assurance. Desire must *be* desire. Consecration must *be* consecration. Determination must *be* determination. All his consciousnesses must be *genuine.* His knowledge must be *sure,* else every subsequent step will be vitiated by the uncertainty of the initial movements. And this necessity applies both to his knowledge of the conditions to be complied with in obtaining the remedy, and to his own fulfillment of those conditions.

5. He can never be satisfied with anything short of a *positive assurance of cure.*

Whether that assurance be derived as a logical conclusion from premises consciously known, or as an inference from conscious fruits within, or accepted as the testimony of another, in either case, it must lack no element of positive affirmation. The soul instinctively desires and calls for a conviction of cure as clear, decided, and unmistakable, as it has had of disease and want.

6. Yet all the foregoing processes of conviction, convincement, desire, consciousness, and assurance, must be subject to the modifications of thought and feelings naturally induced by changes of physical conditions. Anything more or less than this would inaugurate an essentially different era of probation, as well as remove man from the operation of those forces that play upon him through his physical organism; in short, would make him something other than *man*.

3. *There is another class of principles which relate to the Tempter.*

No view of the work of salvation can be complete that does not embrace the energies of the Arch-adversary and the principles which control their activity.

1. The first principle, both in the order of nature and of importance, is, *unmitigated hostility to the work in all its phases;* a hostility, not merely of taste, or habit, or feeling, but of the deepest repulsions of the nature; a hostility so elemental, comprehensive, and exclusive, that its instinctive feelings are antipathies—its spontaneous utter-

ances are condemnatory—its ever-springing influences are antagonistic.

2. Hence follows, *his pre-inclination to frustrate the work,* in each of its several stages of conviction, convincement, desire, faith, consciousness, and assurance, by any means of deceit, falsehood, crimination, over-reaching, discouragement, unbalanced extremes of feeling, stupefaction, irritation, etc., that may be within his power. Constituted as men are, and situated as they are amid so many occasions for the play of his energies in these directions, the opportunities for the gratification of his hostile inclinations are not infrequent. Consequently, the importance of recognizing the principles which direct his movements cannot well be over-estimated.

CHAPTER V.

THE LAWS IN ACTION.

On page 4 laws were defined as the uniform methods of action of physical, mental, and spirit forces in the production of the facts of Christian Holiness. The question now arises:

What are the laws of Christian Purity? Their classification is already indicated in the definition given. The psychical and spirit-forces often combine in thought-processes so intricately that it is difficult, and perhaps unimportant to distinguish them. Hence we adopt the common method, and consider such combinations, as well as the purely psychical, under the following heads:

1. *Mental.*
Under this head we consider—
1. *Laws of* NORMAL *development and action.*

(1) The first of these is, the recognized dominancy of the regulative faculties, viz., reason, conscience, and judgment.

Linked as we are to the world by chains of direct material causation, it is not surprising that the sensuous part of our nature is emphatically impulsive, and, as such, blind and unreasoning. Its primary spontaneity is toward indulgence, and its strongest instinct pleads for gratification. Desire is law. Craving is license. But man is destined for a higher sphere than the merely sensuous; hence certain faculties are given to him, by which desire may be curbed and indulgence subjected to rule. Reason, conscience and judgment, standing over against temptation, impulse, and desire, are commissioned regulators of their capricious movements, and authorized expounders of the law of innocent gratification; and only in their supremacy can there be harmonious development of being.

(2) Habitual use of the mental faculties, each in its own appropriate sphere, is another law of normal mentality.

The axiom of science, that possession of a faculty is an indication of designed use, applies as well to man as to beast, and as well to each separate faculty as to the totality of his nature. Man's mind is a complicated arrangement of parts, like a well constructed machine, each part having a distinct office to perform, and being nicely adjusted to the whole, so that from the individual movements of the parts shall result a combination of effects which shall accomplish the object of the designer.

And, in this co-ordinate movement it is important that each part shall do its own work, and that only. The minute-hand of the watch may by excess of energy not only travel its appointed rounds with unslackened speed, but may likewise drag the hour-hand with it around the dial. All such appropriation of the work of another by any part can have but an unfavorable result. So, each mental faculty has its sphere in which it alone is the proper worker; and so nicely are their adjustments fitted, that any disturbance of their normal relations must result disastrously.

Of course, it will be understood that these remarks apply only to the use of faculty *upon occasion*. We are so circumstanced that an uninterrupted use, during our working hours, of *all* our faculties, is impossible. But, when occasion requires its use, if one remains dormant it is in violation of a constitutional law of our being, and like all other transgressions of fundamental laws, must find a disastrous result, greater or less, according to the relative importance of the faculty and the interests involved.

(3) The testimony of each faculty, unimpeachable within its appropriate sphere, is the third law of correct mental action.

The truth of this proposition lies at the basis of all reliable investigation of the phenomena of life. If it be once conceded that the testimony of a faculty when in a state of health, and occupied within its appropriate sphere—both as to the character of its exercise and its subject-matter—can be invalidated by the doubts of any other faculty, there is endless confusion introduced at once, and uncertainty, broad as the possible questionings of a universal skepticism, results.

This law will be found to have a most important bearing upon certain phases of religious experience, hence it should be carefully noted and well remembered.

2. *Laws of* ABNORMAL *development and action.*

(1) The first that meets our attention is what may be called the law of *perversity;* as when the control of the regulative faculties is overcome by those inborn tendencies, or by those acquired habits which assume the mastery over men in the ratio of their strength, and domineer the will with a savage recklessness that knows but the single law of blind, greedy, headstrong indulgence.

Nor are these tendencies and habits all. Our natural appetites—angel ministers turned into tempting devils—have sworn fealty to tendency and habit both, and the alliance of the unholy trio constitutes the wild, maddened host of our impulses toward wrong, which, in concert with the temptations of the external world, wage an unremitting warfare against the spirit.

Opposed to these are the conscience—the faculty which recognizes obligation, whose vocabulary is comprehended in the phrases "ought" and "ought not," and which tells us how, from our stand-point, to avoid guilt; the judgment—the discriminating faculty, rendering its decisions formed out of the elements furnished by the whole nature of the man, and his surroundings, according to the presentments of reason; and the will—peremptorily deciding in view of the motives presented on the one hand by the temptations and impulses, and on the other by the conscience and judgment.

The conflict, then, has come to this: on one side are ranged temptations and impulses; on the other, conscience and judgment; while above all, in magisterial supremacy, sits the will—a Moses giving victory to Israel with extended arms, but conquest to Amalek with hands not upheld. Now, it sometimes happens that these regulative faculties are so perverted that it is impossible for them to control the nature.

The external world is as the key-board of the piano in juxtaposition with the internal world of connecting hammers ready to smite the strings. It is thus a grand solicitor and the mind is the solicited, and, as such, it yields mechanically in instantaneous response to the solicitations. In the first motions of response, it is as helpless and innocent as any other mechanism. Yet its true sovereignty consists in this, that it need not surrender itself to the potency of the impulse.

In the days when persecution was considered a mark of Christian zeal, there might have been seen in one of the torture halls of the Inquisition one Zeno upon the rack; and as they turned the crank, and the muscles began to stretch and the joints to give, the terrible pain of that racking process cried out through every nerve: "Recant!" But his conscience protested, and his will coincided, so he nobly bit off his tongue and spit it out in the face of his executioners, lest in the hour of weakness it should betray him. From that heroic display of the sovereignty of will down to those weaker exhibitions when its greatest power is seen only in this, that it raises a feeble and insufficient protest against the impulses, but only enough to prolong the struggle which ends at length in defeat, there is a gradation from the high to the low, which shows that sovereignty fading out by degrees, down to absolute inefficiency.

It may seem that it is true only of idiots and lunatics that there are tendencies in some natures which are an overmatch for the regulative faculties; yet, they may co-exist with large intellectual power, as in the case of the two Coleridges, father and son. The elder Coleridge was an opium-eater, and his will was so powerless that he was obliged to have a constant attendant to keep him out of mischief; yet he had an almost peerless intellect. He begged his friends to send him to an asylum, where he might be kept out of evil. His son inherited his imbecility of will, and plunged into evil without apparently trying to resist it. He seemed to yield spontaneously to the temptations that were presented, and thus records his sad experience:

> "Oh! woeful impotence of weak resolve,
> Recorded rashly to the writer's shame:
> Days pass away, and Time's large orbs revolve,
> And every day beholds me still the same.
> Till oft-neglected purpose loses aim,
> And hope becomes a flat, unheeded lie."

Is it possible to conceive of a man in a more wretched condition than this—with an intellect that thoroughly understands its unfortunate position, and yet with a will so imbecile that when the temptation comes it is welcomed by the perversities of the nature, and no power within to resist it?

Should the question be raised here: "Whence came this bent of nature?" The answer is: These perversities are largely *physical*. They belong to the brain, were inherited from parents, and have been modified by experience, until they powerfully affect social and religious life. Suppose a boy, in handling a hatchet, strikes it deep into the fleshy part of his hand. The wound will heal, but let that boy live to be a hundred years old, and nature will not forget to repeat the scar every day of his life. That is to say, there is something impressed upon the vital force of that boy's body, which makes it, instead of building up the tissues of that particular portion of the hand as those of the same portion of the other hand are built, build it up in the form of a scar, and it never forgets to do so. So men come into this world with their brains scarred through and through by the blows that have been inflicted upon them by the vices, indulgences, and proclivities of their parents; and it is little wonder that they become twisted into all sorts of abnormal deformities; and as little that they tend to evil as naturally as sparks fly upward. Such physical perversities cause the mental forces, that must play through them, to give forth the discord that the piano would give if its adjustments were incomplete or disarranged.

(2) *Irregularity* is another law of abnormal mentality, and it consists in the habitual disuse, or excessive use of certain faculties.

Much less injurious than the foregoing form of perversity, unless it be carried to such an extreme as to have become perversity, it is nevertheless to be deplored, because habitual disuse is almost always attended with more or less loss of power, while excessive use always tends toward perversion. The ideal man is one whose faculties are all in use, upon occasion, and in such regulated exercise that only harmonious action results. Very far below this ideal we are constrained to be; nevertheless, the laws of our best life must be deduced from such an ideal, and it needs but a glance to show that the irregularities under consideration detract ruinously from the character of perfect mentality.

This law often manifests itself also in the shape of *confusion and encroachment*; as when one faculty or set of faculties arrogates to itself the functions of another. When men speculate upon established truths, following the bent of an erratic Imagination where only the most disciplined Reason should tread, they introduce confusion and discord, not only within the realm of accepted doctrines, but likewise amid the certitudes of their own intellectual processes.

Imagination has its function, and a noble one it is; but her fiery spirit and tireless wings but poorly qualify her for the slow, toilsome, plodding, matter-of-fact investigation by which truth is sometimes reached, or the relentless sifting and rigid questioning by which it is established. Here Reason, Judgment, and Experiment must speak; while in the realm of creative genius, and sometimes in the domain of inspired Hope, Imagination may soar to her loftiest flights, and flash the most gorgeous hues from her sun-bathed wings, and man shall be blessed as he gazes.

So Emotion has its sphere, and Will its place;

but Emotion, either sobbing or shouting, must not usurp the throne of Will, nor yet the mandates of the Will attempt the ebullitions of the Emotions. Each must do its own work, and that only, is the perfect law of life; and any departure from this is the imperfect and damaging law of abnormalty.

(3) A law kindred with the foregoing is that of *distrust;* as when the validity of the affirmation of one faculty within its own sphere is called in question by another outside of its sphere. E. g. When the Fears dispel the comfort of well based Hope, or Hope presumes upon the possession of good that Caution hesitates to endorse, or Caution occasions distrust where Reason gives good assurance of security, or transient Emotions assume the voice of Consciousness of general state, or Consciousness of present general condition invalidates specific acts of Faith.

Distrust of a positive affirmation of any faculty by reason of the mere suggestion of any other faculty, is one step towards lunacy; whether the particular field in which that distrust roots itself be mental or spiritual.

2. *Spiritual.*

The spiritual being only the mental in its infinite and eternal relations to the Supreme, differs only in its adjustments from the mental in its finite relations. Therefore, the only elements to be added here are those which are derived from the contact of the mental with the Divine.

1. *Laws of* NORMAL *spiritual development and action.*

(1) Acceptance of Christ as the only and all-sufficient Savior.

The atonement is a fact apprehended by the mind, by means of the Holy Scriptures, as bearing upon its relations to the Supreme. The sufficiency and exclusiveness of that fact are cognate conceptions. These conceptions demand appropriate treatment, which can be nothing less than the fulfillment of the obligations arising from their possession. Hence the acceptance of Christ is the first legitimate law of spiritual development.

(2) Complete submission to the will of God, is another law of normal spiritual action too apparent to need argument or illustration. We therefore pass it by to dwell upon another equally manifest, yet practically so frequently called in question, that some delay upon it may be a benefit to the reader.

(3) Entire consecration to the work of God.

"Ye are not your own, but are bought with a price; therefore glorify God in your bodies and in your spirits which are his," is the claim which the supreme Jehovah makes in his Word upon all; and it is a claim that Philosophy recognizes as valid and imperative upon those who would honor their relations to God. *His work* is not only the development of a righteous character in the individual, but the *use* of that character in the procurement of a like development in others. Hence, entire consecration to God's work implies not only a definite and unconditional surrender to his will, but the use of all legitimate means for self-growth, and the faithful application of the energy developed within to the culture of those around; and this, too, not as an occasional outflow of extra-stimulated zeal, or as a temporary gratuity of gratitude or sympathy, but as an abiding, normal law of Christian life.

To suppose anything short of this as the law, is to throw the whole decision upon poor private judgment, warped by prejudice, cramped by indulgence, and distorted by proclivities to sin. It is easy to see that such a non-authoritative, ever-varying standard of appeal could yield but one result, viz., declining piety, and service of diminishing worth.

Such a law, honored, will of course result in a corresponding *state*. The state, it is true, will begin in a consecratory *act;* but it can never find its complete fulfillment in a single act, however comprehensive; it must pass on into a consecutive, on-flowing disposition and attitude of the nature.

(4) Reliance upon the guidance and sustainment of the Holy Spirit.

Too blind and helpless to travel unaided in the way of life, the Christian ever feels the need and rejoices in the privilege of being guided and upheld by the Divine Comforter. Few promises of the sacred Word come with more sweet and welcome refreshment to the spirit than those which assure of direction and help. To take the hand extended to lead us, and lean upon the arm reached out for our support, is felt to be not only a favor of sonship but a condition of continued discipleship. Hence it may be regarded as another law of spiritual development.

(5) Procurement of the special helps of grace.

The law last named contemplates only the ordinary assistance of the Holy Spirit in the common experiences of the Christian. But times of extraordinary pressure come to all, when circumstances seem in league with the powers of darkness to imperil the spirit—when simply to "*hold on*" requires a concentration of energy and a desperateness of determination that mark the crisis hours of destiny; and, when such hours come, the heart casts about for reserve-forces, and calls imploringly for the residue of the Spirit.

Then is realized the value of the *special helps* which come only in response to the cry of special need. Then, if such help be not received, wreck or loss inevitably ensues. So imperative, therefore, is the necessity for unusual grace, that its acceptance and use at such times may legitimately be regarded as still another law of normal Christian activity.

There is another class of laws in spiritual life, directly opposite to those named, which correspond with the laws of disease in the physical organism. These may be called—

2. *Laws of* ABNORMAL *spiritual development and action.*

(1) Partial acceptance of Christ; *i. e.*, an acceptance which lacks completeness when considered in relation to the largest needs of the suppliant—an acceptance which does not measure to the length and breadth of want.

In so far as such deficiency exists, there must be a corresponding repression of the vital forces of Christian life, and a consequent appearance of abnormal symptoms of worldliness, selfishness, or passion, that clearly indicate unhealthfulness within. The only antidote to these natural conditions is reliance upon the indwelling Christ—

a reliance which is in itself the condition and the measure of his helpful grace.

(2) Rebellions against God's will.

As submission to his will is the most thorough touchstone of Christian character, it is not surprising that when that character is defective in any of its important elements, or lacking in their proportionate strength, it should reveal the fact by protests and murmuring in times of suffering or loss, and wilful resistance to extreme obligations. This is one of those bad uniformities of depravity, occurring in connection with insufficiency of grace, that we feel constrained to note as a law of abnormal spiritual development.

(3) Defective consecration to God's work—which is a consequence of the partial acceptance of Christ, and whether a cause or consequence of rebellion against God's will—is an almost unvarying uniformity of all inferior types of discipleship, so clear and decisive that it may be regarded almost as a thermometrical scale of fidelity.

Hence, in the most successful evangelism, the prime effort is to secure a renewed consecration of believers to the work of God. And even when this is not formally done, such consecration, as a matter of fact, almost always precedes any marked efficiency in Christian life. It is evident, therefore, that a defective consecration must ever be regarded as a source of weakness, so full of peril that its causative power demands recognition amid the abnormal laws under discussion.

(4) Partial self-guidance, and self-dependence.

These are only varying phenomena of an unhealthy spiritual condition, yet so constantly occurring in nearly all unsatisfactory religious states that they may be deemed indices of a corresponding law of diseased immaturity.

(5) Neglect of the proffered aid of the Holy Spirit.

Since by that aid alone all progress is made, and since the rapidity of the progress is largely dependent upon the aid actually accepted, it follows that if it be spurned or neglected there must be a corresponding diminution in the results achieved. But with active forces of evil within, and ever-pressing evils around, the forward movement cannot be retarded beyond a certain degree without a result speedily fatal to its subject. Hence the neglect of the proffered aid of the Holy Spirit may be regarded as one of the initial retrogressive conditions of a questionable experience.

(6) Mental instability.

That some are so unfortunate as to be vacillating and unreliable throughout most of their lives, is a matter of fact that few will dispute. That such do become Christians with high ideals and noble purposes, must be admitted upon the common rules of evidence. That their subsequent, otherwise unaccountable aberrations, spring from constitutional infirmity, it is but charitable to conclude. Such infirmity, wherever found, becomes a divergent force of unmeasured power, revealing itself in a law of instability, referred to in the parable of the hearers who had "no root within themselves."

(7) Excessive mental bias.

Strong prejudices of judgment and proclivities of desire, with great obstinacy of will and excessive fervor of zeal, often constitute, either singly or compounded, a state, the perpetuated characteristics of which indicate a uniformity of evil that may be appropriately termed a law of abnormal development. Doubtless this and the foregoing class are only species of the mentally abnormal groups referred to on pages 78, 79, but it should be noted that on page 84 it was affirmed that the spiritual is only the mental in certain relations; hence we should expect to find the abnormalities of mind projecting themselves within the spiritual realm and manifesting themselves by like characteristics there.

(8) Bodily infirmities.

Here we enter upon a broad field of investigation, the importance of which has been strangely overlooked by most writers upon this subject. Not that all physical ailments are to mark their subjects as under the laws of abnormal spiritual development; but that there is a sufficient number of such which proclaim their anti-spiritual power with sufficient persistence and uniformity to entitle them to appear in the category here referred to, will be made evident as we proceed to discuss—

3. *The physical laws of the subject.*

These may be classified thus:

1. *Laws of* NORMAL *development and action,* as when each organ healthfully performs its function.

(1) Healthful *respiration;* including air enough to thoroughly fill the lungs, and of sufficient purity to completely oxygenate the blood. This, of course, supposes the absence of mechanical restraints upon the natural movements of the ribs and diaphragm, and the freedom of the atmosphere from noxious effluvias and baneful malarias. The reader will note that we are considering *laws*—not easily attainable conditions; hence no regard can be had in the statement to the constraining force of circumstances.

(2) Normal *circulation;* unimpeded by injurious local compressions or the constrictions of

chilling exposures, and undisturbed by the congestions of over-wrought activity; a circulation that bears upon its strong and even tide all the effete matter of the system for elimination, and a rich burden of nutritive aliment for assimilation, amid the wasting structures and tissues of the frame.

(3) Adequate and balanced *nutrition*; so that the wastes of life shall be continuously repaired just when they occur, and thus no parts be enriched by the poverty of others, but all alike built up in strong and equal equipoise.

(4) Well regulated *activity*. It is the law of our being that organic integrity shall be preserved by functional activity. Hence partial activity, or general activity with long intervals of inaction, are both, by their organic re-actions, seriously detrimental to sound health either of body or mind.

(5) Timely and sufficient *protection*. Exposure is a common incident of life, and always opens a possibility of evil. Hence the necessity for protection both timely and sufficient; for sufficient protection lagging behind the exposure, or a timely protection insufficient to shield from the exposure, are alike in vain.

2. *Laws of* ABNORMAL *physical development and action.*

(1) Of disturbance of function.

A. Either diminished or excessive functional activity. Either of these states may exist in any organ of the body; and as the organs are so numerous, the functional disturbances to which we are liable are so various and multiplied that an extended work upon pathology would be requisite to describe them. For our present purpose it is enough to call attention to the fact that, in all physical deviations from the normal condition, every step of the departure is as much under the control of the not-living forces of matter as the processes of health are of vital organization; hence there is strict propriety in affirming the existence of *laws* of abnormal physical action, and in the appropriate place it will be seen how intimately this fact is related to the subject of this volume.

B. Sympathetic disturbance of other functions. Such are the relations of the several parts of the body through the great sympathetic nervous organization, that serious functional derangement in one organ can scarcely exist without greater or less sympathetic disturbance of other functions. Hence, it often happens that a local change or cessation of function—as, for example, torpidity of the liver—will produce general physical prostration, and mental lassitude, finally resulting in spiritual depressions and almost hopeless despondency.

(2) Of organic change of functional product.

The mischief begun in functional derangement, and extending itself sympathetically to other organs, does not stop there. A function supposes some product of functional activity. If the function be abnormal, the product will be likely to be abnormal also, and the divergence may be more than in degree; the product may be organically different, and hence utterly unadapted to fulfill its original purpose. E. g. Secretions that in a state of health are lubricating, in a state of disease may become painfully and even dangerously irritating. So, the thought-product of the brain, under the influence of narcotics and stimulants, may vary, from the rose-tinted visions of the hasheesh eater, bordering in vividness and beauty upon the celestial sphere, to the demon-haunted madness of the victim of delirium tremens, presenting—if the term may be thus applied—an organic change of functional product exhibiting the tremendous power of diseased action.

(3) Consequent organic changes elsewhere.

The changed product of functional activity is not necessarily neutral or harmless. On the other hand, it is often virulent to such a degree that it corrodes or decomposes tissues with which it comes in contact, thus producing organic degeneration at a distance from its own place of origin. E. g. The acrid secretions of the mucous membranes of the nose and head, excoriating the nostrils in some cases of catarrh.

(4) Of inheritance, producing abnormal natures.

The reader should constantly bear in mind the fact that the word abnormal is used in this connection only in the technical sense of opposition to the highest and best natural. E. g. Disease is abnormal not in the sense that it is not in and of nature, but that it is not the *best* of nature, since the best is health. So these abnormal constitutions are not out of or beyond nature, but are specimens of its imperfect, or at least not best work.

Heredity is the tendency inhering in all living beings to repeat themselves in their descendants, in structure, special characteristics, abnormal conditions, and acquired modifications. In the whole range of science there is scarcely a more important subject of inquiry than this. That there are fixed and definite laws of inheritance, cannot be doubted. That these laws profoundly affect the physical and mental status of all men at the beginning of their lives, and of multitudes throughout the whole of their lives, is equally certain. That some of them have been ascertained, and are practically applicable to the purposes of life, seems settled from the use made of them in the breeding of domestic animals. That they affect, to a greater or less extent, not only the feasibility, but the *possibility* of Christian attainments, may be a startling statement, and is one that well merits careful investigation.

"Heritage has in reality more power over our constitution and character, than all the influences from without, whether moral or physical." (*Burdich*)

"Heredity is but one form of that ultimate law which by physicists is called the conservation of energy, and by metaphysicians, universal causality." (*Ribot,* "*Heredity,*" p. 391.)

That physical and moral degeneracy is a frequent result of vitiated parentage, is the testimony of all intelligent writers upon this subject. Concerning the inheritance of a tendency to drunkenness, "M. Morel, who has investigated this subject more profoundly than any living writer, says: '*I have never seen the patient cured of his propensity whose tendencies to drink were derived from the hereditary predisposition given to him by his parents. . . .* I constantly find the sad victims of the alcoholic intoxication of their parents in their favorite resorts—the asylums for the insane, prisons, and houses of correction. I as constantly observe amongst them DEVIATIONS FROM THE NORMAL TYPE OF HUMANITY, manifesting themselves, not only by *arrests* of *development,* and *anomalies* of *constitution,* but also by those *vicious dispositions* of the *intellectual order* which seem to be deeply rooted in the organization of these unfortunates, and which are the unmistakable indices of their *double fecundation in respect to both physical and moral evil.*'" (*Naphys* "*Transmission,*" etc., p. 213.)

"The habit of the parent becomes the almost irresistible instinct of the child; the voluntarily adopted and cherished vice of the father or mother becomes the overpowering impulse of the son or daughter; the organic tendency is excited to the uttermost, and the POWER of WILL and of CONSCIENCE IS PROPORTIONATELY WEAKENED." (*Elam,* "*Physician's Problems,*" p. 5.)

"Acquired habits in several successive generations become permanent, and assume the character of instincts." (*Sir Benj. Brodie, Mind and Matter,* p. 212.)

"Acquired and habitual vice will rarely fail to leave its trace upon one or more of the offspring, either in its original form or one closely allied to it. (*Elam, P. P.* p. 5.)

"A recent writer in the *Psychological Journal* says: 'The most startling problem connected with intemperance is, that, not only does it affect the health, morals, and intelligence of the offspring of its votaries, but *they also inherit the fatal tendency, and feel a craving for the very beverages which have acted as poisons on their systems from the commencement of their being.*'" (*Ibid*, p. 40.)

Insanity is universally recognized as an hereditary disease, but writers differ as to the proportion of the insane whose malady originated in heredity. Mr. Esquirol says one-half, while Dr. Burrows estimates eighty-four per cent. as correct; Moreau of Tours, ninety per cent.; Ribot, from thirty-three to fifty per cent., and Dr. Maudsley says "less than fifty per cent.;" and accounts for this diversity by the statement: "Not insanity only in the parents, but any form of nervous disease in them, epilepsy, hysteria, and even neuralgia, may predispose to insanity in the offspring, or, conversely, insanity in the parent may predispose to other kinds of nervous diseases in the offspring." (*P. and P. of Mind*," p. 243.)

Feuchtersleben, as quoted by Elam, represents the insane tendency as manifesting itself "on the psychical side by passiveness in thinking, in feeling, and in *willing*; and on the physical side by predominant erethistic [morbidly excitable] vital debility." And M. Morel adds to the physical signs of its presence, "*the strangest and most incomprehensible aberration, in the exercise of the intellectual faculties, and of the moral sentiments.*"

The practical out-come of all this is thus given in the forcible language of Dr. Elam, p. 58: "If moral liberty means anything beyond a formula without interpretation, it means the power of choosing and acting, according to the dictates of judgment, conscience, and will, in opposition to impulse and temptation. The impulse and the temptation being increased, and the faculties of judgment and will, and the dictates of the conscience, being both relatively and absolutely diminished, it follows necessarily that, in proportion to these changes, moral liberty is invaded, its powers curtailed, and responsibility to some extent modified. *These are precisely the variations which we observe.* . . . In one we have an impulsive nature, in which, between the idea and the act, there is scarcely an interval; in another, the proneness to yield to temptation of any kind —a feeble power of resistance, inherited either from the *original or acquired* nature of the parent; in a third we have imbecile judgment; in a fourth, an enfeebled, vacillating will; in a fifth, or in all, a conscience by nature or habit torpid, and all but dormant. All these are the normal representatives of an unsound parentage; and all are *potentially* the parents of an unsound progeny; in all is moral liberty weakened; in all is responsibility not an absolute, but a relative idea." "All moral qualities are transmissible from parent to child, *with this important addition*, that, in the case of vicious tendencies or habits, the simple practice of the parent becomes the passion, the mania, the all but irresistible impulse of the child." (*Physician's Problems*, pp. 58, 59, 84.)

THE LAWS OF TRANSMISSION AND HERITAGE.

These have been stated variously by different writers, while there is substantial agreement as to the facts. Our own classification is—

A. *Uniformity.* By this law, the individuals of a race through successive generations preserve their race-peculiarities of structure, type, and function. "Every living thing produces its own kind and no other." (*Cook.*) To this law, Mr. Cook's "co-equal" law of heredity may undoubtedly be referred, since the reproduction of about equal numbers of the two sexes is a part of their function. This law of uniformity is based upon the fact that between the parent and the germ of the child exists a physical and psychical likeness induced by the primary operation of the life-force in generation.

B. Duplication, (the "direct heredity" of Cook who here follows Ribot,) by which individual peculiarities are transmitted in any of the following named classes, namely:

a. Physical peculiarities of structure or function. Of these, Th. Ribot in "*Heredity*," pp. 36–45, has given numerous examples in respect to touch, sight, hearing, taste and smell. Maupertius, *Œuores*, vol. 2 : letter 17, citing a case of sexdigitism which persisted through four generations, shows that by the law of probabilities the chance that a man with six fingers will have a child with six, is as 20,000 to 1. That his grandchild will have, is as 4 millions to 1, and that three successive generations will be thus is as 8,000 millions to 1.

Many authors, particularly Burdach, have insisted with considerable weight of argument that there is an invariable connection between physical and moral heredity; that the parent who transmits the one does also the other. Limiting the physical just here to cranial developments, we are disposed in the main to accept the doctrine.

Dr. J. M. Fothergill, in "*The Maintenance of*

Health," pp. 175-180, says: "The chief classes into which inherited constitutions are divided are five: the gouty, the strumous, the nervous, the bilious, and the lymphatic." In the *gouty*, the frame is well developed, nutrition good, muscles firm, respiration and circulation good, mental powers vigorous, courage high. Their danger is a tendency to live too well and so develop inherited tendencies to disease. In the *strumous*, the skeleton is not well developed, muscles not firm, vital force defective, mind quick, apt to be precocious, not enduring. These are in great danger of tubercle, and are unsuited to a life of self-denial and privation. In the *nervous*, the person is small, of restless activity, well proportioned, and powerful beyond the promise of their muscles. They have great brain power and endurance, are quick, excitable, and feel keenly. Their danger is in overtaxing their strength, and nervous affections induced by excessive activity. In the *bilious*, the physique is good, dark haired, dark hued skin, often active and powerful, but gloomy. Their danger is, derangements of the digestive organs, and great susceptibility to malarial influences and the depression of hot climates. In the *lymphatic*, the frame is large, muscles soft and flabby, and greatly wanting in energy—the opposite of the nervous in physique and mentality—unsuited for a life of exertion, and decidedly inclined to passive hemorrhage, and to diseases of a low chronic type; even more than the bilious susceptible to external influences.

b. Organic, or nervous diseases. Ribot, "*Heredity,*" pp. 123-131, has given abundant illustration that hallucination, monomania, suicide, mania, dementia and idiocy are transmissible. See also Elam, "*Physician's Problems,*" pp. 25, 41, for cases of hemorrhage, and consumption, and pp. 53-54 for various nervous affections.

c. Special tendencies or aptitudes to certain modes of action, derived from the acquired habits of parents. Speaking of oinomania, or dipsomania, Dr. Elam says, p. 72: "The habit of the parent, when inherited, does not appear in the child *merely as a habit,* but in most cases as an irresistible impulse, a disease." In confirmation of this position he quotes M. Morel as referring to cases in which was "*a complete abolition of all the moral sentiments,*" and then he adds: "The offspring of the confirmed drunkard, rich or poor, *will inherit either the original vice or some of its countless protean transformations.* . . . With regard to other vices . . . whatever has a tendency to lower the physical, intellectual, or moral tone of the parent, has a tendency, *seldom lost,* to exert a disastrous influence over the future well-being of the child. Let the source of degeneration be what it may, the offspring will inherit a body or mind bearing traces of imperfect fitness or balance, which sooner or later will assert its presence and power." Ribot, "*Heredity*," p. 116, cites the case of the gypsies for whom Borrow translated the Gospel of St. Luke into Romany. They accepted the book and carried it about their persons as a talisman when they went to steal.

d. Mental traits. For many illustrations of hereditary memory, imagination, poetry, painting, music, science, etc., see "*Heredity*" by Ribot, pp. 52–80. Fothergill's "*M. of Health*," pp. 173–4. Dr. A. K. Gardner, "*Our Children*," pp. 40–42. For heredity of will, see Ribot, pp. 94–107.

e. Sentiments and passions. Illustrated at length by Ribot, "*Heredity*," pp. 83–94. See also "*Heredity*," ("Science Tracts, No 2,") pp. 6–8, S. H. Platt, for some remarkable instances in the State of New York. Rev. Dr. T. D. Witherspoon relates the following incident:

"During a season of religious awakening a young lady called at my study in deep distress. She had come to me because she loved her own pastor so much that she could not bring herself to make a confession which she knew would grieve and horrify him. It was some terrible sin, at the very thought of which she shuddered, but the nature of which her lips refused to tell. Some time passed in fruitless efforts to secure from her the confession which she had come to make, and her agony seemed every moment to increase. At length I took my Bible, and opening to the twentieth chapter of Exodus, asked her to place her finger upon the commandment she had broken. Slowly, and with a great struggle, she lifted her finger and placed it upon the words, "Thou shalt not take the name of the Lord thy God in vain." Knowing her gentle birth, her pious parentage, her religious training, and the refined society in which she moved, I was amazed, and inquired how it could possibly be. Then she told me all. Her mind was filled with *horrid oaths;* oaths which, as she protested, she had never heard from human lips, and which, therefore, could only originate with herself; oaths too horrible to be repeated, and yet obtruding themselves upon her *even in the midst of her devotions*, until her soul seemed to be but a depository of the most blasphemous and revolting formulas of profane swearing. She had heard oaths at times, but never such as those which were constantly coming into her mind. Long did this distressing state of mind continue, and even after it was gone, and peace and relief were found at the cross, there remained the unsolved mystery, until, on a certain occasion, some gentlemen were speaking in my presence of the father of this young lady and of his recent decease, when one of them remarked that he had heard many men swear, but had never known any man who could *invent* such *strange and awful oaths*, and utter them with such terrific emphasis, as did this man in his *earlier and irreligious days*. To my readers must be left the connection between this extraordinary profanity of the father and the terrible visitation in after years upon his lovely and accomplished daughter."

C. Diversity. If *both* parents transmit somewhat to their offspring, a necessary consequence of the admixture of these two in the production of one, must be diversity. And that both must impart something must be supposed from the fact that there are established laws of transmission. According to P. Lucas, approved by Ribot, the child should be the exact mean of his two parents by the ideal law. This diversity may manifest itself in one or more of the following ways, namely:

a. In species and varieties. Variations from the common type are well known facts in nature, and are constantly produced by the interbreeding and special cultivation of domestic animals by man. Hence this form of diversity needs no extended illustration.

b. In nervous diseases; e. g., insanity, epilepsy, Saint Vitus' dance, hysteria, neuralgia and catalepsy sometimes change their character in the descendants and become lunacy, idiocy, or some form of nervous disease different from that which afflicted the parents.

"A simple neuropathic [diseased nerve] state of the parents may produce in the children an *organic disposition* which will result in mania or melancholy—nervous affections which in time may give rise to more serious degeneracy, and terminate in the idiocy or imbecility of those who form the last links in the chain of hereditary transmission." (*Dr. Morel.*)

Speaking of the children in houses of correction, Dr. Legrand du Saulle says they are "whimsical, irritable, violent, with little intelligence, refractory, ungovernable and incorrigible—children of old men, blood relations, drunkards, epileptics or lunatics, or, as is more frequently the case, the father is unknown, and the mother is scrofulous, rickety, hysterical, a prostitute or a lunatic." Dr. Elam adds: "Hysteria or chorea, in one generation, may become imbecility, mania, or epilepsy in the next or third. Insanity in any form in the parent may be represented in the offspring either by a similar affection, by sensory disorders, (as deaf-dumbness, etc.,) by epilepsy, by hysteria, or by vague and undefined weaknesses or perversions of judgment, capacity or will, which we call *unsoundness of mind.*" ("*P. Problems,*" p. 57.)

c. In transmission of temporary states of parents when they become such, called by Cook the "initial law of heritage." The transmission of the actual and momentary state of the parents at the instant of conception has been treated at length by Lucas, Morel, Quatrefages, and others, and is an unquestioned fact in heritage. "There is no doubt whatever, that under such circumstances, [when a child was conceived at the time the father was partially intoxicated] the child is pretty sure either to be *idiotic*, or to have epileptic fits, or to be of a feeble mind and irritable nervous system." (Napheys, "*Transmission of Life,*" p. 186.)

Dr. Combe, as quoted in Fernald's "*First Causes of Character,*" pp. 33, 34, gives an account of a soldier who at an entertainment danced and sang with a young woman the whole evening. They then left the cottage and after an hour were found together in a glen in a state of utter insensibility. The consequence was the birth of an idiot, who at six years of age was utterly incapable of making even signs, and did not know any human being. Both parents were intelligent, but their intellects were almost totally eclipsed by intoxication, and the darkness was transmitted as a heritage of doom to their child.

The popular tradition that illegitimate children are handsomer and more healthy than others, undoubtedly originated in the notion that they are more likely to be "love children," hence inherit the temporary state of their parents. However much of truth there may be in this, there is even greater probability that such children will inherit the unrestrained *impulse to indulgence* exhibited by *both* their parents in the act which gave them being.

D. Impressional Heredity; as when the emotions of the mother during the period of gestation produce corresponding modifications, mental or structural, in the child. This is called by Cook "pre-natal heredity."

To the writer it seems probable that the "reversional heredity" of Cook and Lucas and the "atavism" of Ribot and other authors—words used to express the inheritance of qualities from grand-parents instead of parents—should be referred to impressional heredity, as it is far more probable that some impressions on the mind of the mother cause the modification, than that a distinct law should exist comparatively so seldom operative. For the same reason, the "pre-marital heredity" of Cook, the same as the "heredity of influence" of Ribot, by which is designated likeness to a first husband in the child of the second husband, should also be referred to the law of impressional heredity, and especially as no case has come to our knowledge even among animals, much less the human race, where such inheritance has come through the *father*, *i. e.*, where the child of the second wife has resembled the first wife. Burdach *Traite de Physiologie*, p. 243, gives examples of the law, but they are all of progeny of females resembling earlier consorts. Still further, and for the same reason, Mr. Cook's "collateral heredity," the same as Ribot's "indirect heredity," by which he distinguishes resemblances to uncles, aunts, cousins, etc., should be likewise classed under impressional heredity.

Impressional heredity differs from the law of duplication chiefly in this, namely: The former registers transient states of the mother, while the latter transmits abiding conditions; and duplication may be from both parents, while impressional heredity is from the mother only. "One of the most distinguished authors on idiocy," says Fothergill, "lays it down as a rule that of idiots the largest proportion are first-born children, the imperfection here representing the disturbance of the mother's nervous system in her first conception." He also cites the discovery by Sir James Simpson of a dark brunette, the eldest child of blonde parents, whose other children were all blondes. The explanation was this: The mother had in early life been too intimate with a black butler, and the secret had been kept buried for years, until the resemblance of her child to the lover of the dead past rather than the real parents excited inquiry. "Children have been known to be thrown into fatal convulsions, by nursing a mother while she was in a phrenzy of anger. Is it then unreasonable to believe that the physical condition and mental emotion of the mother, during the nine months of gestation, must have a material influence upon the constitution and mental attributes of a creature, which lies close under her heart? For a time this child is part and parcel of herself, every nutriment comes from her veins, she gives it being, and can it be doubted that she gives it physical character, mental stamina, and nervous energy?" (Gardner, "*Our Children*," pp. 54, 5.)

Dr. Carpenter cites a case in point in *Physiology*, Sec. 723. M. Foster, *Physiology*, p. 698, says: "Speaking broadly, the fœtus lives on the blood of its mother, very much in the same way as all the tissues of any animal live on the blood of the body of which they are the parts." Prof. Dalton, *Human Physiology*, relates the case of a child born with a defective ear from a *dream* of the mother that she saw a man with such an ear; and Prof. Lewis of Bellevue Hospital, as cited by Mr. Cook, refers to the case of a child born with the figures of a watch dial on the white of its eye, from the longing of the mother to see a watch. "The faculties *actively used* by the mother during pregnancy, rather than those lying latent and part of her original character, will be found prominent in her offspring." (Georgiana B. Kirby, "*Transmission*," p. 10.)

A striking illustration of this law of transmission came under the observation of the writer. The parents were wealthy and of unusual culture and intelligence, and resided in a large city. During one of the mother's periods of gestation, friends visited them from a distance, and while there one of them was suddenly seized with a contagious disease that, if known, would have compelled immediate removal to the hospital. The heart of friendship revolted at the thought, and instantly closing their house—as if away in the country—that mother nursed her friend through the long hot weeks of an exceptionally warm summer, tormented with the double fear of the death of her patient and the discovery of her unlawful deed in harboring her, until at last she had the satisfaction of seeing complete recovery reward her self-sacrifice. Her own confinement soon followed with an apparently bright and healthy boy, but as the months rolled away the painful conviction was forced upon the parents that their child was nearly daft. Years have gone by, and the poor boy still lives, amiable, affectionate, and bright in some respects, but utterly incapable of self-care or even of mastering the common principles of reading and writing. No other adequate cause can be assigned than those terrible weeks of voluntary imprisonment and desperate battling with disease while feeding the life-springs of the coming child.

Georgiana B. Kirby, "*Transmission*," pp. 25-48, gives several examples of impressional heredity of great significance to every mother.

E. Recurrency; or the tendency to return from variation to the original type.

"In all natural departures from the original type, due to special causes, there is a constant tendency to return to the type." ("*Physician's Problems,*" p. 10.) Probably from the overmastering *persistence* of the law of uniformity.

Napheys refers to a special modification of this kind, thus: "There is a force resident in our nature by which the diseased organization tends to return to health. This benign healing force, this *vis medicatrix*, . . . is ever influencing the effects of inheritance. . . . The law of inheritance is a certain but not an invariable one. Its force must not be overestimated. . . . Diseases are but perverted life-processes, and have for their natural history, not only a beginning, but a period of culmination and decline. . . . By time and rest, that innate *vis medicatrix*,

> 'Which hath an operation more divine
> Than breath or pen can give expression to,'

reduces the perversions back again to the physiological limits, and health is restored. To this beneficent law we owe the maintenance of the form and beauty of our race, in the presence of so much that tends to spoil and degrade it. . . . The effects of disease may be for a third or fourth generation, but the laws of health are for a thousand." ("*Medicine in Modern Times,*" Dr. Gull, p. 187.)

MODIFYING FORCES.

We must not overlook the fact that these laws of inheritance may in any case be largely affected by one or more of the following *modifying forces*, namely:

(*a*) The influence of one parent in counteracting the influence of the other in transmission. "The influence of one parent upon the other in counteracting or intensifying the degree and the certainty with which the physical qualities of one or both are transmitted must be borne in mind. If the same defects be possessed by each parent they will be quite certain to appear in the children. If only one parent be affected, some or all the children may escape the inheritance. . . . It is most fortunate that the tendency of a disease to propagate itself by inheritance is often overpowered by the stronger tendency of a vigorous constitution to impress itself upon the offspring." (Napheys, "*Transmission of Life*," p. 206.) Says M. Girou: "Acquired capacities are transmitted by generation, and this transmission is more certain and perfect in proportion as the cultivation has extended over more generations, and *as that of one parent is less opposed by that of the other.*"

(*b*) The union of the influence of both parents in the transmission of the same peculiarity. The quotation above scarcely needs the sanction of Fothergill's statement: "The children of both parents of a certain diathesis (predisposition to disease) will have that diathesis very marked; ... will be doubly, nay quadruply apt to suffer from it." ("*Maintenance of Health,*" p. 184.) The fact is too evident to need further confirmation.

(*c*) Any influence that gives temporary dominancy to the forces of diversity as against duplication, or *vice versa*. Under this head may be classed all those cases where an exalted diversity of duplication or impression blesses the offspring of bad parentage, and thus improves the family, as well as those cases where diseased or passionate conditions of diverse or impressional heritage curse the family with degenerate children.

(*d*) Any habitual subjection to causes that antagonize recurrency, such as education of the children of drunkards in habits of tippling, bad conditions of life surrounding the children of consumptives, and habitual examples of crime before the eyes of the families of the vicious classes. Such habitual subjection to conditions which tend only to fix the inborn perversity, will be almost certain to overcome the law of recurrency, and perpetuate the degeneracy to that point where it cures itself in sterility and extinction.

(*e*) Spontaneous variations, if such there be, as distinct from impressional heredity. It seems difficult to account for some facts of variation, especially in domestic animals, upon any other hypothesis than that of spontaneous divergence. Yet, it is hardly satisfactory to the philosophical mind to admit a law *so apparently lawless*, especially when the occasions which seem to require it are so few. Hence, we associate the supposition of spontaneity with the "impressional heredity" which we know exists, but the full power of which can never be measured, with the doubt attached.

The case cited by Dr. Parsons, (and quoted in Herbert Spencer's *Principles of Biology*,) by Ribot, and others, of two negro slaves living on the same Virginia plantation is curious and well attested, as the girl was sold to Admiral Ward and by him was taken to London and exhibited before the Royal Society when she was fifteen years of age. Husband and wife were both black. Her child was white. In fear of her husband's anger at her supposed unfaithfulness, she tried to hide the babe from him by darkening the room. He procured a light and examined the child. Afterwards he said to his wife: "You were afraid of me because my child is white. I love her all the better on that account. My own father was white, although my grandfather and grandmother were both as black as you and I. Although we came from a country where white men were never seen, yet there has always been one white child in our family." Quatrefages, as quoted by Ribot, affirms that similar phenomena have occurred even in Africa. Ribot, "*Heredity*," p. 195, quotes as facts of spontaneity those called by Zimmermann "exceptions in temperament;" e. g., "a man who suffered extreme agonies when his nails were clipped; another, when his face was washed with a sponge. For some persons coffee is an emetic, jalap a constipant. Hachre could not eat more than seven or eight strawberries without falling into convulsions, and Trisot could not swallow sugar without vomiting."

Still we incline to the opinion that all variations from type—seemingly spontaneous or otherwise—if not included under some law already named, are to be referred to the law of impression; and we find that Ribot makes the sound distinction between facts of spontaneity and a law of spontaneity—admitting the first, denying the second.

If inquiry be made for the *cause* of transmission, the answer is, "Physiology regards every living body as an aggregation of multitudes of cells, each of which has a vitality of its own, possessing three essential properties of life, namely: nutrition, evolution, and reproduction.

Mr. Darwin's theory is, ("*Variations*," vol. 2, chap. 17,) that each cell reproduces itself. . . . This theory of physiological tramsmission is applied psychologically on this wise: Force, or nerve-power, exists in every nerve-cell. These cells, reproducing themselves, impart their own special characteristics to the progeny, and thus give mental heredity." ("*Heredity*," S. H. Platt, p. 3.) "The cause of heredity," says Hackel, "is the partial identity of the materials which constitute the organism of the parent and the child, and the division of this substance at the time of reproduction." Psychological heredity has its cause in physiological heredity.

The practical working of heredity is seen in national facts. E. g. The physical degeneracy of the French is accounted for by an able writer on the ground that parental affection and medical science prolong the lives of multitudes of weakly children to become the parents of a weaker generation.

The deterioration of Spaniards is attributed by Galton to the fact that by martyrdom and imprisonment the nation was drained of free-thinkers (*i. e.*, independent thinkers) at the rate of 1000 persons annually for 300 years.

" Heredity transmits, preserves, accumulates." In its *constitutional* and *temperamental* union, however, is its chief interest in this investigation. The constitutional diatheses have already been sketched. The temperaments are thus discriminated by S. R. Wells. ("*New Physiognomy*," pp. 100-109.)

The motive, or mechanical, distinguished by predominance of bone and muscle, strong tendency to angularity, firmness of texture, energy and endurance. The ancient Romans, and the Americans are types of this temperament. The Diana of Grecian sculpture is a classic example of the same slightly modified in art. Its excessive development is seen in the Farnese Hercules, and the dying gladiator.

The vital, or nutritive, characterized by predominance of the vital organs, rotundity, great activity, love of play, impulsiveness, brilliancy rather than depth, good livers, fond of stimulants. This is the temperament of women. Extreme, it becomes the lymphatic constitution.

The mental, or nervous, marked by predominance of brain and nerves, slight frame, slender neck, high forehead, chest not large, great sensitiveness, vividness and intensity. This is the temperament of literature, art, and poetry. Morbid, it runs into the nervous diathesis indicated by quickness and intensity of sensation, suddenness and fickleness of determination and morbid impressibility.

Now, if we remember that physical perfection consists in a *proper balance* of the temperaments, and that by heredity the nervous diathesis conioins with the mental temperament, or the vital temperament with the lymphatic diathesis in a *double heritage of bad conditions,* and even sometimes a double diathesis transmits a *quadruple leverage of degeneracy,* we can but feel how hopelessly imperfect is the organism with which such unfortunates begin the tremendous struggle of life

CHAPTER VI.

THE RELATION OF THESE LAWS TO PERSONAL RESPONSIBILITY.

By personal responsibility is meant individual answerability to God;—that upon which the rewards and penalties of eternity will be predicated.

No more momentous question can possibly be asked concerning anything than whether it affects personal responsibility; and, if so, to what extent, and in what manner. With deep solicitude, therefore, we approach this branch of our subject, and in humble dependence upon the enlightenment of the Holy Spirit, seek the answers without which this philosophy must be incomplete and unsatisfactory.

1. *Personal responsibility is modified by two principles, namely:*

1. There must be sufficient *knowledge* (or opportunity for knowledge) of the facts or relations concerning which responsibility is affirmed, to constitute a basis of obligation.

Children cannot be held accountable for violations of the rights of property, until sufficient knowledge has been acquired to give a comprehension of the distinction between mine and thine, as a matter of *right*, and not merely of possession.

The *heathen* cannot be held accountable for not loving and serving Christ, of whom they have never heard.

So the *Christian* can only be answerable for the subject matter of his knowledge, not for that which he does not know, unless culpable neglect of opportunities for enlightenment can be justly charged upon him.

2. There must be sufficient *power in himself* to act *according* to his *knowledge,* or, to *avail himself* of such *gracious helps* as will enable him thus to act.

To *know,* and not to have the power to *do*, would be to load life with an insufferable burden, confuse the practical judgment as to the extent of possible obedience, and appall the heart with a sense of the injustice of the obligation involved.

To *love* the Being who has imposed such an obligation, would be impossible. He might be feared and served; but once thoroughly establish the conviction in any mind that He holds it accountable for that which it cannot do, either aided or unaided by grace, and that conviction is the tomb of love. The human mind is so constituted that to suppose it capable of loving one in the relation of Creator so flagrantly unjust, is to suppose it so mal-adjusted to itself that its deepest instincts can be emptied of power, and its purest and most sacred love become enamored of the eternally unlovely.

God seeks the love of men; therefore he can never impose such obligations as will be an impassable barrier to their confidence and affection. Hence, obligation only up to the limit of natural or graciously aided ability, is one of the most unvarying principles of his moral government, and one to which all men, unless biased by theological creeds, give their instant and hearty assent.

That this principle has a broader application to the subject of Christian holiness than at first sight appears, will be evident when we come to treat of the practical relation of the abnormal physical states to the possibilities of Christian attainment.

2. *These principles applied to the laws of Christian Holiness.*

1. The sufficiency of *knowledge.*

Applying this principle to the third mental law of perversity, viz.: "The testimony of a faculty impeachable within its appropriate sphere,"—it is evident that if that testimony be thus open to doubt, knowledge is to that extent vitiated. E. g. Suppose that the verdict of conscience as to personal guilt be not true to fact, or the consciousness of penitence be chargeable with delusion, or the purpose of obedience be mixed with deception, or conscious reliance be illusion, or the presentations of the judgment concerning the reality of God's claims be fictitious; in any of these cases, and in many others that might be named, knowledge made up of such misleading elements must necessarily prove defective and most probably ensnaring.

Therefore, if there be a duty of Christian holiness, that obligation implies the prior validity of the normal mental law of the trustworthiness of faculty-testimony. And conversely, if this law be accepted, the basis of the obligation is laid in the mind thus accepting, if there be anywhere any materials for a philosophy of the doctrine, or any convincing evidence of its truth.

2. The sufficiency of *Power*.

The first mental law of abnormal development has been stated (p. 78) to be that of "Perversity"—*i. e.*, the regulative faculties non-controling. The sixth and seventh abnormal laws of spiritual development (pp. 90, 91) are "mental instability" and "excessive mental bias." The eighth, "bodily infirmities" (p. 91), may be coupled with the fourth abnormal law of physical development and action, viz: "The law of inheritance producing abnormal natures." (p 96.)

To all these, this principle of power as related to personal responsibility, directly applies. It will be observed, however, that the principle is alternative; *i. e.*, it assumes sufficient inherent power to act according to knowledge, *or* sufficient inherent power to accept the offer of gracious help thus to act.

Now, if the mental instability be too great for either exercise of this power with sufficient continuity to constitute a state of salvation, there certainly can be no obligation to abide in that state. So, if mental bias be so excessive as to constitute an intellectual deformity irreducible to the symmetry of a sanctified condition, there can be no duty incumbent upon such to find that condition. So, if bodily infirmities have grown to the stature of a distinct species of abnormal humanity; or, if the law of inheritance has developed such a species—*a lack of this power being the chief characteristic of the species*—it is plain that the obligation to *use* such deficient or absent power can in no case rest upon such unfortunates.

Were science sufficiently keen-eyed, there is no doubt that in all such cases the physical condition of the brain or other nervous centers would be found to be at fault, and in many instances— *far more than we think to be the case*—there is practical subjection of the personality to the heredity or to the specific characteristics of an acquired unhelmed condition, even when the degeneracy has not reached to the extent of recognized insanity.

The following propositions could doubtless be maintained: (1) There is a condition of the nervous system (more or less transient) in which *impulse is the only law*. (2) In persons of a certain temperament and constitution, that condition may be induced by circumstances. (3) Their responsibility for conduct while in that condition is graded by their previous responsible conduct in relation to the circumstances which induced the condition; *i. e.*, if they voluntarily placed themselves in the midst of these circumstances, knowing their exposure, they are accountable for results, and *vice versa*. The unfortunate victims of dipsomania (alcoholism) may be cited as illustrations.

Hence it follows that if there be laws of Christian holiness binding upon such persons, those laws must be modified to suit the disabilities of those to whom they are applied. Moreover, as a further consequence of this view, God must be as well pleased with their gracious attainments under their special laws, as he is with the larger attainments of the better-favored under their higher laws. But his pleasure in their attainments should be considered entirely apart from the general standard of Christian consistency with which the conduct of other believers is compared. The injustice of requiring such constitutionally imperfect ones to display the same exterior that we have a right to demand that others shall exhibit, is much like that which would expect of a shattered epileptic the strength and service of a stalwart son.

All this may be theoretically accepted by some who at the same time demur to its practical utility. But if such will remember that impossibilities grade downward in life through almost insurmountable difficulties, very great and grave hindrances, warring antagonisms, damaging impediments, and simple obstructions to spiritual progress, they may be led to consider that somewhat is due to the weary and almost hopeless toilers up the slippery steeps that lie just this side of impossibility, more than to those who are never called to climb such perilous places. Without indorsing the extreme views of the following extract, we insert it as expressive of the justice-born questionings that will arise in reflective minds, and which we think are better answered, in point of principle, by the graded responsibility above named, than by the poet's hypothesis concerning Paul.

THE CHEMISTRY OF CHARACTER.

John and Peter, and Robert and Paul—
God in his wisdom created them all;
John was a statesman, and Peter a slave,
Robert a preacher, and Paul was a knave.
Evil or good, as the case might be,
White or colored, or bond or free,
John and Peter, and Robert and Paul—
God in his wisdom created them all.

Out of earth's elements mingled with flame,
Out of life's compounds of glory and shame,
Fashioned and shaped by no will of their own,
And helplessly into life's history thrown;
Born by the law that compels men to be,
Born to conditions they could not foresee,
John and Peter, and Robert and Paul—
God in his wisdom created them all.

John was the head and the heart of his State,
Was trusted and honored, was noble and great;
Peter was made 'neath life's burdens to groan,
And never once dreamed that his soul was his own;
Robert great glory and honor received,
For zealously preaching what no one believed;
While Paul of the pleasures of sin took his fill,
And gave up his life to the service of ill.

It chanced that these men in their passing away
From earth and its conflicts, all died the same day.
John was mourned through the length and breadth of
   ' of the land;
Peter fell 'neath the lash of a merciless hand;

Robert died with the praise of the Lord on his tongue;
While Paul was convicted of murder and hung.
John and Peter, and Robert and Paul—
God in his wisdom created them all.

Men said of the statesman—"How noble and brave;"
But of Peter, alas! "He was only a slave;"
Of Robert—"'tis well with his soul, it is well,"
While Paul they consigned to the torments of hell.
Born by one law, through all nature the same,
What made them differ, and who was to blame?
John and Peter, and Robert and Paul—
God in his wisdom created them all.

Out in that region of infinite light,
Where the soul of the black man is as pure as the white—
Out where the spirit, through sorrows made wise—
No longer resorts to deception and lies—
Out where the flesh can no longer control
The freedom and faith of the God-given soul,
Who shall determine what change shall befall
John and Peter, and Robert and Paul.

John may in wisdom and goodness increase,
Peter rejoice in infinite peace,
Robert may learn that the truths of the Lord
Are more in the spirit and less in the word,
And Paul may be blessed with a holier birth
Than the *passions* of *men* had *allowed* him on earth.
John and Peter, and Robert and Paul—
God in his wisdom created them all.

The special laws under which these unfortunates are held may be hypothetically stated—thus:

(1) That of conscious integrity of purpose to live up to the limited possibilities of the case;—a sliding scale, adjustable to all degrees of weakness, and obviously within the compass of every person concerning whom Christian responsibility can be affirmed. In its application it is not necessary that the subject himself shall be wisely able to discriminate as to exact shades of possibility, but in a general way shall be conscious of a purpose "*to do his best.*"

(2) An honest and habitual effort to carry that purpose out in conduct;—another sliding scale, admitting very diverse degrees of practice, yet perfectly adaptable to the infirmities of this special species of our race.

True, these laws might be affirmed as applicable to *all* men; so they are; but those whose regulative powers are normal, and adequately balance their impulsive and emotional nature, can square their conduct by more specific rules, hence the "mint anise and cummin" of the law are for their observance.

2. In the possession of sufficient knowledge and power, the normal laws of Christian Holiness *sweep through the entire field of personal re-*

sponsibility. If the reader will return to Chapter V, pp. 74-77, 85-88, and read carefully with this inquiry in mind, namely—Which of these mental or spiritual laws can be eliminated and leave the *doctrine* intact ?—he will at once perceive the importance to be attached to each several law, and will be constrained to admit that if any one of them can be supposed to be of no binding obligation, that supposition vitiates the whole; for, if the regulative faculties are not dominant, others adverse to holiness are; if faculties may trench upon the sphere of each other, confusion, and not certainty, must result; if the testimony of the faculties may not be relied upon, we have no testimony; if acceptance of Christ may be dispensed with, we need no Christ; if submission to the will of God be not imperative, then rebellion may be piety; if entire consecration be not enjoined, then we have self-rights superior to God's rights; if reliance upon the guidance and sustainment of the Holy Spirit be not necessary, then are our deeply-felt and oft-asserted weakness and blindness frauds in the interests of godliness; if procurement of the special helps of the Holy Spirit be of no account, then are we competent of ourselves to exorcise all the demons of habit and inheritance that possess us.

Surely, no sincere hater of sin will take a position leading to such logical results. We are therefore entitled to urge respect for all these laws upon every Christian conscience, and to emphasize the urgency by all those yearnings after increased goodness and longings for practical efficiency which should characterize every child of God. Here, if anywhere, the least suggestion of conscience should be heeded. Here, rather than any elsewhere, should the Spirit's drawings be felt and followed.

Even this much may be readily granted by some who, however, would pause here and hesitate to admit that the like reponsibility attaches to the laws of normal physical development. (pp. 92-93.)

It seems so easy to assume that our bodies are our *own*, to be dealt with as we please within the limits of ordinary prudence, that a Divine claim like this sounds harsh and exacting, namely : "Ye are not your own ; ye are bought with a price : therefore *glorify God* in your BODIES and in your spirits, which are his." Can he be *glorified* in the needless violation of any of the normal laws of physical development ? If so, then is his house "divided against itself." Then also is the authority of nature abrogated by her most honored sons, and human caprice—ravenous as appetite and fickle as fancy—is enthroned to sway a scepter of lawlessness over the empire of these " temples of the Holy Ghost."

Yet a moment's consideration of the possible functional or structural results that might ensue from the customary violation of any of those laws —as well as of the practical impossibility of fixing any standard of responsibility in relation to these things, if violation may, innocently, at any time, or in any respect, be arbitrarily decreed without the justification of a superior moral interest—must convince every candid mind that here in the realm of physical laws, as well as in the domain of the mental and spiritual, responsibility must be predicated. That is, the man who has a body under the dominion of certain laws of health, and whose body, by the culpable violation of those laws, will react injuriously upon the mental or spiritual states, or both, is under the same principles of obligation to honor the laws of health that he is to obey the laws of spiritual development ; and for the all-sufficient reason that he transgresses the laws of spiritual life in the very act of breaking those of physical health.

We readily concede the practical impossibility of an absolute observance of the laws of health. The exigencies of our every day life constrain us frequently deliberately to sacrifice them to what we deem higher interests, and when we do so, as we may conscientiously and righteously, the act undoubtedly falls within the compensative scheme of Providence, by which loss in one direction is made up by gain in another. But this is entirely different from those culpable violations which can plead no higher interest in extenuation of their guilty being—mere indulgences, the demand for which springs out of the roots of self-life and carnality, and the enjoyment of which fortifies selfishness, and encourages a spirit the exact opposite of the self-denying spirit of the gospel. Such indulgences can *never* be habitually enjoyed without a corresponding spiritual loss; therefore there is *no room for them within the area of Christian liberty.* Not that they necessarily utterly alienate the life of God, nor yet are incompatible with a considerable degree of saintliness, but that they are defects which increase the friction, while they also reduce the strength of the spiritual machinery—*without correspondingly reducing the work to be done.*

PART II.—CHAPTER I.
THE THEORY OF CHRISTIAN HOLINESS.

1. Man has a three-fold nature—spirit, soul and body. (pp. 29, 30.)

2. The spirit has a trinity of faculties or endowments utterly differentiating it from the soul; namely, consciousness, conscience, and intuitions of futurity. (pp. 30, 31.)

3. Its consciousness affirms the existence of its conscience and intuitions, and also its universal judgment, from these, of moral obligation.

4. Its consciousness affirms that the demand which its conscience makes is that of *perfect obedience.*

5. Its intelligence apprehends a law of obedience, given in the word of God, and a future existence conditioned in kind, at least, if not in duration, upon conformity to that law.

6. The consciousness affirms that in attempted conformity, as well as in a common disinclination to *seek* conformity, very grave difficulties are met, called depravities. (pp. 7-14, 22, 24, 27.)

7. Its intelligence finds revealed in God's word a plan of grace, by which, upon certain conditions, supernatural aid is proffered in overcoming these difficulties.

8. A careful analysis shows that after that plan is accepted in regeneration, and while the state of justification continues, those difficulties inhere entirely in the soul and body.

9. Hence the proper and legitimate work of Christian life is—

1. To *continue* in a *regenerated* state.

2. To seek the *complete complemental condition of soul and body*, in which they shall be the fit, unobstructing and unperverting instruments of the pure spirit.

3. That complemental condition to be reached,

(1) *By substituting out* every old habit of soul and body which is inimical to the spirit's purity, or obstructive of the spirit's will, or untruly representative of the spirit's condition; and

(2) By securing the *revolutionary power* of the *Holy Ghost*, by which instantaneous changes, structural or otherwise, are made in answer to the desire and faith of the human spirit, equivalent —in its removal of embarassments, and in its substitution of right processes of thought and feeling —to the substitutional work of years of discipline.

4. That complemental condition to be maintained by securing a fresh application of the revolutionary power of the Holy Ghost upon every occasion when the process of development. or

change of circumstances, brings to the foreground of conflict any revealment of want of harmony between the spirit and its instruments—soul and body. (pp. 26, 27.)

10. In the progress of Christian life, when previously *acquired habits,* such as the use of intoxicants, tobacco, opium, etc., are found to oppose spirituality, testimony too multitudinous to be disregarded, and too intelligent and respectable to be impeached, proves beyond question that the revolutionary power of the Holy Spirit can in a single instant *remove the appetite,* so that thereafter not a desire shall be felt for the old indulgence.* Usually, this is only done in answer to the faith of the subject; but the writer has known at least one instance (in the case of an intimate friend) where the desire for tobacco was eradicated in answer to the prayers of another, unhelped by any prayer or religious consideration of any kind, or any preparation, either mental or physical, on the part of the subject, so far as he has been able to discover after a critical review of his mental states at the time.

* "*The Power of Grace,*" by the author of this treatise, is a record of numerous examples of this truth, to which the reader is referred for further information upon this point. Dr. Daniel Steel, in " *Love Enthroned,*" has a good chapter (the 12th) upon this subject, largely made up of extracts from Rev. W. H· Bool's justly celebrated "Wonders of Grace."

11. When diseases are found detrimental to piety by reason of the peculiar nervous conditions which they produce, or for other reasons, the power of the Holy Spirit can instantaneously extirpate them in answer to the *divinely suggested* and *divinely helped* prayer of faith.

What we mean by "divinely suggested" and "divinely helped," is precisely what Paul meant when he said, "Likewise the Spirit also helpeth our infirmities," (what infirmities?) "for we *know not what we should pray for as we ought;*" (how then does He help this specialized infirmity?) "but the Spirit itself maketh intercession for us with groanings ($στεναγμοις$, sighings) which cannot be uttered." (Rom. 8 : 26.) But how does that help us? "And he that searcheth the hearts" (wherein these Spirit-excited groanings are) "knoweth what is the mind ($φρόνημα$, inclination) of the Spirit *that* (margin) he maketh intercession for the saints *according to the will of God.*" (Verse 27.)

Now, turning to 1 John 5 : 14, 15, we read : "And this is the confidence that we have in him, that if we ask ANYTHING *according to his will*, he heareth us." How? By his knowledge of the spirit's inclination. What then? "And if we *know* (by our spirit-excited groanings) "that he hear us, WHATSOEVER *we ask*, we know that we have the petitions ($αιτημα$, *asking*) "that we desired of him." It certainly is not unreasonable to suppose that what God has *promised*, he will sometimes thus help our prayers for.

The next verse, 1 John 5 : 16, gives a *divine application* to the verse above, "If any man see his brother sin a sin which is not" (by divine decree) "a sin unto death, he shall ask" (as above, "according to the will of God") and he shall give him" (the suppliant) "*life* for those" (not for this sinning brother only, but for *all* for whom he *thus* asks) "that sin not unto death."

With this express and, so to speak, constitutional provision in the gospels for physical cures written 50 years after the Savior's death to Gentile converts and believing Jews, as if on purpose to project the privilege off into post-apostolic times, we turn to James, and find that 30 years before he had given this explicit direction: "Is any among you afflicted? let" (expressing either privilege or obligation) "him pray. Is any mourning? let" (privilege or obligation again) "him sing psalms. Is any sick among you? let" (again precisely the *same* privilege or obligation as in both the other cases) "him call for the elders of the church: and let" (the *same* obligation or privilege in this case) "them pray over him, anointing him with oil in the name of the Lord;

and the prayer of faith shall save ($\sigma\omega\zeta\omega$, *heal, recover*) the sick, and the Lord shall raise him up: and if he have committed sins, they shall be forgiven him." (Jas. 5 : 13-15.)

This was an *apostolic direction* given to the *church* "amid the twelve tribes scattered abroad," either commending a certain privilege, or enjoining a certain duty in a class of cases particularly specified. Thirty years roll by, and the patriarchal apostle John, gathering in his eye the necessities of further authoritative announcements of privilege or duty, gives to the world the passages above cited, enlarging the privilege of faith-cures from that of church-elder's intervention and anointing, to that of Spirit-helped *prayers alone!* Thus the privilege passed from apostolic times into the world's later history.

12. When the natural appetites, by reason of excessive development, or deficient regulative power, prove a hindrance to spiritual growth, the Holy Ghost can so re-adjust them to the trusting spirit that they shall become instruments of delight either *indulged* or *denied*, as may be found in God's order.

No more fatal foe to deep spirituality exists than is found in the bad conditions and unfavorable relations of the sexual appetite; yet multitudes suffer on most of their lives, scarcely or

ITS PHILOSOPHY AND EXPERIENCE. 143

never suspecting the real cause of their trouble. Yet a prudish public sentiment refuses to allow the discussion of the subject in works designed for general circulation, utterly banishes it from the pulpit and the school-room, and even from the sacred confidences of the pastorate, and therefore remands it to be locked up amid the mysteries of medical lore, or to be treated in those *special works* which are read only by the few, largely because, not having the advantage of the regular book trade, they can only be circulated by special means and therefore are necessarily too expensive to secure very general circulation. To attempt its discussion in these pages would be to invite the condemnation of the suicidal sentiment referred to, hence all that the writer can do is to direct the reader's attention to judicious special works of this class, by a perusal of which he may complete the theoretical view but glanced at in the beginning of this paragraph.*

---

* The writer knows but two books which present this subject in full from the *gracious* stand-point indicated above. There are many that contain good advice, faithful warnings, etc.; but "*Princely Manhood*" for men, and "*Queenly Womanhood*" for women, are the only works, so far as the author knows, that present the *height* of *Christian privilege* in this all-important matter. These works are having a large circulation, as *helps* in the foreign missionary fields of India, Burmah, etc.

13. If a conjecture may be hazarded as to the *modus operandi* of the Holy Spirit's revolutionary processes, it is this: Recalling the statement on pages 49, 50, that the human spirit stands in the relation of a higher nerve-center to the peripheral ends of the nerves of communication of the hemispheres of the brain, sending down its influences through all the complicated mechanism of which the hemispheres are the crown; so, we suppose that the Holy Spirit in connection with the human spirit stands in the same relation. And, just as the nerves may be made pathways for the electric current to travel over, intensifying nervous energy as it goes, so that the powerful shock of a forty-cell galvanic battery annihilates apparently incurable sciatica at a blow; so, the current of Divine Life sweeping down upon the hemispheres, enveloping the sensori-commune and the cerebellum, piercing through the medulla, thrilling along the spinal cord, and permeating and exalting every nervous center, may instantaneously dash neuralgias of habit and sciaticas of desire clear out of the organisms in which they had rooted apparently for life.

14. Whether the Holy Spirit instantaneously changes the form or structure of brain-cells or blood-corpuscles from a habit-diseased to a cured condition, as when the drunkard is in a moment disenthralled from the tyranny of desire; or whether the dominancy of the *law of emotion* (or its physiological equivalent) holds the desire in abeyance until new and healthful forms and structures are built up, it is of little consequence to know. But the law of emotion—as an equivalent for a sanctified soul, in its operations upon those who die spirit-regenerated but soul and body unsanctified—*is* of importance as a seemingly correct hypothesis to account for entire holiness in heaven, following only partial sanctification on earth, with no intermediate work of grace.

This law of emotion may be thus stated: A person may be suffering intense longings for some habitual indulgence, narcotic or stimulant or passional, and while thus tortured with ungratified desire, the sudden cry of "fire!" from his dwelling, or of "murder!" from the street, will instantly sweep the desire from his consciousness, nor will it obtrude itself again until the cessation of the suddenly aroused emotion of fear or solicitude. The emotion of joy—as by the unexpected return from sea, of a long-mourned son—has the same expulsive power. Were the preponderance of the emotion long enough continued, there can be no doubt that new processes would be instituted which would effectually eradicate the habitual desire, and substitute something akin to the prevailing emotional experience.

May it not be that when all the partially sanctified Christians of earth shall stand amid the radiant glories of the celestial land, and listen to the rapt hallelujahs of the angelic hosts, and gaze upon the wonders of that holy sphere, their own souls meanwhile thrilling with the ecstatic conviction of everlasting safety and unspeakable blessedness —may it not be that *then* an emotional experience shall seize and possess them, so absorbing, so continuous, so supreme, that all soul-desires shall be not merely quiescent, but rapturously harmonious? And may it not be that in view of this certainty of soul-sanctification by the law of emotion, God graciously proposes to give to all his saints a complemental body-sanctification in the resurrection—($\sigma\omega\mu a$ $\pi\nu\varepsilon\upsilon\mu a\tau\iota\varkappa o\nu$) spiritual body. (1 Cor. 15 : 44.)

15. Applying to this subject the "pan-genesis" hypothesis of Darwin (see H. Spencer's *Principles of Biology*, Vol. I., p. 65) the inference seems clear that sanctified parents may transmit godly predispositions to their offspring; for, if "gemmules springing from modified nerve-cells are transmitted to the descendents," each "possessed of force, of life, of tendencies" (Ribot, "*Heredity*," 279), and if this be a reasonable explanation of the possibility, universally admitted, of the "*acquisition of new instincts*," and if "psychological heredity has its cause in physiological heredity, and this in turn has its cause in the partial identity of the materials constituting the organism of both parent and child, and in the division of this substance at reproduction" (which is pangenesis), then modifications effected by spiritual forces are just as transmissible as any other, and even more than most others, because they are associated with the deepest convictions, the strongest emotions, the most changeless principles, the supreme purposes, and the dominant habits of the parent's being. What Dr. Bushnell called the "out-populating power of the Christian stock," is thus seen to have a basis in the very method and process of heredity.

Yet it should be borne in mind that this godly heritage is, at best, only a predisposition toward righteousness—not righteousness itself, not even so strong in its leanings as to be necessarily or even greatly preponderating—a predisposition like any other; subject to all the modifying influences of association, education, personal volitions, constitution and temperament, yet a *vantage ground of motive* in the desperate struggle with sin—an anchorage of nature to the right amid the storms of passion—a mortgage of God upon the domain of self—a linking of parental fidelity to oneness of destiny!

16. Possible sanctifications may be divided into three or four classes; namely:

1. *Normal;* when under the ordinary operations of grace, as stated on pp. 25-27, the whole nature is harmonized into conformity with God's will.

2. *Neuropathic;* (borrowing a word from pathology) when the reactions of the nervous centres are so far impulsive and emotional, that *health*—not grace—is their proper regulator; and when conjoined with this pathological condition, is a state of spiritual aspiration and purpose which, under more favorable physical conditions, would ensure normal sanctification.

3. *Super-normal;* when a diseased condition obstructive to normal sanctification is removed in answer to the divinely-suggested prayer of faith, and the sanctification of the nature is concurrent with the cure.

4. Theoretically, we are inclined to name *Emotional* as still another *possible* species, even in this world; for it is possible to conceive such circumstances of religious emotion, so long continued, and so unalloyed with the movings of old habits of evil, that they might be substituted out before

they could give further evidence of continued existence. But this is of importance only as suggesting how the emotional element may be made subservient to the process of normal sanctification.

Let it be distinctly understood that in all these species of sanctification, the only real purifier is the Holy Spirit. It is the various modifications of his operations that are thus classified.

17. These species of sanctification may be found in the same person at different times, and when so found may be regarded as the equivalent of each other; *E. g.*, one may glide from a state of normal holiness to the neuropathic by the inroads of disease, wherein the *apparent* and *sensible* grace enjoyed seems diminished to a perilous minimum; yet, in God's sight, the neuropathic may be then the full equivalent of the normal. So, he may mount from this deplored condition through the super-normal to almost giddy heights of *apparent* and *sensible* grace, yet never reach a higher mark upon the scale of God's appreciation than when, despite the crazy spasms of lunatic nerves, the Spirit held immovably to its trust.

18. The outward evidences of a sanctified state will be found to be peculiar to the species enjoyed.

1. In the normal, the evidence will consist mainly in the perfect harmony of spirit and de-

meanor with the will of God as expressed in circumstances.

2. In the neuropathic, the outward evidence may be entirely wanting until the subsidence of nervous agitation, and even then may be discernible only to those whose intimacy with the patient enables them to detect the desperate clingings and heroic resignations of the tossed and tortured spirit amid the storms of disturbed energy that dash fitfully over the nerve-highways of feeling and action.

3. In the super-normal, in addition to the normal evidence, there will be the marked contrast between present external and internal healthfulness, and the former external passional and emotional symptoms of the internal disease.

19. By these discriminations, the auther hopes to smooth the way for the *large-hearted charity* that certainly should be exhibited by the possessors of, and the aspirants unto, the sanctifying grace of the Holy Spirit.

If the lines be rigidly drawn, as is too often the case, along the boundaries of the normal experience exclusively, and *all* who do not habitually dwell within them are coldly—not to say in some instances, cruelly—judged to be culpably shortcoming and wickedly inconsistent, it is difficult indeed to preserve the sweet, Christian brotherliness, which ought to characterize this state of grace as its most winning feature, free from a a tinge of the "I am holier" feeling.

"Judge not that ye be not judged," has here an application at once necessary, fitting, and supremely Christly.

CHAPTER II.

OBJECTIONS CONSIDERED.

1. *To assumed facts.*

1. "To the reality of any such experience as Christian holiness in this world."

Answer: (1) It is affirmed as a veritable *personal fact* by great numbers in various denominations, who cite in confirmation of it many Scripture promises, prayers, exhortations, commands, etc., which certainly *seem* to blend into harmonious accordance with the yearnings of the Christian heart, and the testimony of the lips and lives of these confessors of this faith and experience.

(2) The number, character and intelligence of many of these persons, not only entitle their testimony to respectful hearing, but to devout consideration as well, while the acknowledged culture and analytical capacity of not a few of its advocates (professed experimentalists all of them) justly merit the most searching examination of the truth-seeker.

(3) If such an investigation is to be made, we know of no method so rich in promise of success in the interests of truth as a well-conceived and carefully-executed philosophy of the subject. A genuine philosophy of a system of error—as a

scheme of truth—is an impossibility; for long before the asserted facts shall have been tabulated, principles elaborated, forces classified, and laws evolved, the utter confusion of the elements of philosophy will have demonstrated beyond a doubt the hollow falsity of the disguised pretender. On the other hand, if facts are found to range themselves in systematic order; if principles that are in harmony with all related truths have marked clearly defined channels, through which forces of known existence, clearly separable and fully adequate, operate under the guidance of laws of consistent uniformity and constant stability; *then* is there a demonstration of truth, so nearly absolute that he who doubts does so under the impulse of a skepticism too obstinate to be convinced, and too reprehensible to be charitably overlooked. This treatise may fail to reach the ideal of such a philosophy, but truth enough has been found to authorize the confident expectation that some more successful toiler will reach the sun-lit summit in God's good time.

2. "There is an underlying assumption that the consciousness correctly reports the true state of the heart."

Answer: If the objection means anything, it certainly denies the assumption. But let us analyze the statement. (1) What is the "state of the heart" referred to? Evidently, it must be that concerning which responsibility may be affirmed. Any other state of heart has no relation to this investigation. (2) What "report" is expected, or is of any moment in relation to those states of heart? Certainly a true report. (3) Does the "consciousness" make such true report concerning those states of heart for which the individual is held responsible? As we have seen on page 123, the very idea of responsibility implies knowledge; but our internal states are only known to us in consciousness; therefore consciousness must make a true report, else our knowledge is deception, and our responsibility is a delusion.

3. "It is assumed, as a *fact*, that Christians are not made entirely holy by a single act of sanctifying grace."

Answer: It is. It is not asserted that they cannot be, but, as a matter of fact, that they usually are not. "Sanctification up to the measure of light and obligation," is the doctrine proclaimed with emphasis by many—perhaps by most, of the advocates of Christian holiness. But the limitations named, at least imply a possible increase of light and augmentation of obligations, which, if they ever occur, will most surely call for sanctification on beyond the old horizon; and if so, to call that *"entire"* holiness which lay only within the area of the vision, is to leave a more than entire holiness to be attained as the radius of view lengthens; therefore the application of the superlative term to the partial work, glorious and complete as it is within its bounds, seems misleading.

There may be cases in which the work is accomplished at a stroke, and in which the Spirit witnesses to its entireness; but we have misread experience if that is the usual fact.

We have recently met with an experience expressed substantially in these words, *viz.*: "When I consecrated myself, it comprehended everything, conscious and unconscious, present and future, so that I have no struggle now. If anything new comes up it is provided for beforehand, and I simply accept the will of God. *The cleansing was complete.* All that I now have to do is to *accept*, quietly and peacefully. The work of cleansing was done once and forever."

We desire to give full credit to such experiences, be they few or many, and to those who seek purity with a considerable degree of comprehension of what they seek, gained by previous Christian experience, there may be a suggestion of grand possibilities of attainment on the line of *such a consecration* and its complemental faith.

But whether an inexperienced believer, who

knows as yet comparatively little of the nature of "inbred sin," can make such a consecration, not merely *in purpose*, but as an abiding causal condition of spirit, so that its pervasiveness of surrender shall instantaneously penetrate all possible juxtapositions of heart and circumstance as they arise may be open to grave doubt.

It is said that God saves us, "not according to what we can see, but according to his promises." Yes, if he be trusted to save according to his knowledge of our need. But, as a matter of fact, our faith generally comprehends *only what we know;* therefore we do not really believe for any cleansing beyond our knowledge. Hence, if there be "in the depths of our unconsciousness" perversities that will sometime be revealed, either God saves beyond our faith, if the cleansing be entire, or, he leaves this unknown perversity to be treated, subsequently, precisely as he did those which are now embraced within our faith, but were not known to us at the time of our conversion.

4. "The assumption seems to inhere in the very conception of this book, that Philosophy is competent to deal with this question without the aid of Revelation."

Answer: Nothing can be further from the truth. The author cherishes a most profound reverence for the Sacred Word, and all through, the land-marks of our philosophy are fixed by the principles and precepts of that Book of books; but hundreds of works are in existence, treating the subject from that standpoint, while, so far as can now be called to mind, but one has attempted a philosophical elaboration, and that with nothing like systematic thoroughness. If the doctrine be true, a philosophy of it must be possible; for all truth can be systematized after a philosophical method, if only there be enough related facts to furnish the key of the system, since facts are only "the sum of laws," and facts and laws verified become science. Surely, then, it may be permitted to one or two plodders in this hard field to work their way as best they can, and leave to others the sweeter task of plucking the purple clusters that hang ripe and luscious over all their paths.

2. *Verbal.*

"The phraseology employed is unusual, and will not be understood."

Answer: Every author has a right to use such words as he deems best for his purpose, provided that if he *adapts* phrases from other branches of science, art and literature, he uses them only in their legitimate sense; and further, that he clearly defines words of unknown or doubtful significance.

The anatomical, physiological, pathological and

psychological words used in this treatise are most open to the objection. But the author has endeavored to keep the two provisos above named in view; and the intelligent reader who ponders the book (not skims it, as he might a sentimental novel, or even some "popular science" treatise) will find little difficulty in ascertaining the meaning intended to be expressed.

3. *Logical.*

1. "So much concession is made to the materialistic theorists of the age, that the logical outcome of this book must be a direct sense of irresponsibility, or such a diminution of the power of motives as practically to amount to the same thing, on the part of the 'unfortunate' ones who are badly organized."

Answer: At first sight this objection has weight, but the paramount question is—not what *use* perverted organisms may put it to, but— *should the concessions be made in the interests of truth?* We need have no fear that in the end truth will work otherwise than well. God's kingdom is not a "house divided against itself." He will care for the outcome of his own; and truth is his. But the objection is not well-taken, for if the reader will turn to pp. 124–127, he will there see how emphatically a *graded responsibility* is insisted upon, on purpose to meet the case of those who could not be included in the ordinary category of responsibles without the most glaring injustice.

2. " You limit free-will in the proportion that you extend heredity."

Answer: Free-will and heredity are opposite poles of the same truth. Just where the equator lies, may be difficult to determine; but that fact does not impeach the reality of the existence of either pole. For aught that we know, indeed, most probably, the equator is a tortuous line, winding with deep loopings in both directions, and perhaps never long-continued upon a single parallel. It is true that "determinism has become a scientific commonplace," and that free-will, in the sense of "that property of the subject whereby it reacts against the determining causes, and in consequence of this reaction determines certain acts," is hotly denied by many leading scientists of the times.

But Wundt, as quoted and accepted by Ribot —*Heredity*, p. 341—has very clearly shown that there is a "personal factor" back of all determinism,—"that which in us is inmost, and which distinguishes and differentiates us from what is not ourselves, ... by which our ideas, our sensations, our volitions are given to us as ours, and not as the phenomena of something outside of ourselves." (p. 343.)

Ribot attempts to show, however, that even this personal factor has "heredity in its very germ," and despairingly adds: "The question becomes perfectly inextricable—an enigma within an enigma. . . . We touch here upon that region of the unknowable to which every inquiry into first causes invariably leads. Here science ends, and it is as little scientific to hold with the fatalist that there exists in the universe only an absolute determinism, without exception, as to say with their opponents that determinism is only a lower mode of existence, lying outside of and beneath free-will."

But whence the necessity that this antithesis, mechanism and spontaneity—determinism and free-will, shall be reduced to unity? Is it not perfectly conceivable that the limited determinism of heredity may be pre-determined to produce a possible spontaneity amid the inter-lockings of mechanism? In other words, may it not be within the unvarying order of hereditary transmissions that one " personal factor," with freedom as its function, shall be the product of each reproduction?

Dr. Carpenter has arrayed all his wealth of learning and professional acumen in the effort to prove that free-will is the *scientific* deduction from acknowledged facts, while others of equal note have held rigidly to the doctrine of mechanism in physics, mind and morals. Why need we to be disturbed? However far heredity may crowd free-will toward the verge of extinction, so long as it *is*, its responsibility is graded by its power, and if it be in any case pushed over the brink, its responsibility goes with it, and leaves behind only the form of the rose, from which the fragrance and beauty have passed away, while the form is locked in the embrace of forces as fixed as fate.

3. "The use made of the doctrine of heredity is illogical, because education is more powerful than heredity."

Answer: "The special aim of education is to transmit to the *child the sum of those habits to which he is to conform* the course of his life, and of those branches of knowledge which are indispensable for him in the course of his calling; and it must begin by developing in the pupil the faculties which will enable him to make these habits and this knowledge his own. When once it is admitted that education, a long, watchful, laborious training, is indispensable in order to call forth and perfect in the child the development of aptitudes and mental qualities, we must conclude that the heredity acts only a secondary part in the wonderful genesis of the moral individual. The argument is unassailable. That hereditary influences make their mark in predispositions, in fixed tendencies, it were unscientific to deny; but yet it would be inexact to pretend that they implicitly contain the future states of the physical being, and determine its evolution."—*Popular Science Monthly.*

This is certainly as strong a statement as the facts will warrant. While in the main it may be correct, it makes no allowance for those vicious and passional tendencies which so frequently develop, *notwithstanding* the most careful education; so that the real truth seems to be that weak heredities are overborne by training, while the stronger manifest their power even after long-continued adverse discipline. We take the facts as they exist, without regard to relative strength of modifying forces; therefore, if our use of them be germain to our subject, it must be legitimate.

4. "The doctrine of heredity, as here taught and applied, seems to load *parents* with a degree of responsibility fearful to contemplate."

Answer: It does. But if a consumptive father and mother beget a child, does the sad prospect of bringing another human being into the world to suffer and die—appalling as it may seem to them—ever shield the child from the virus of disease? Nature is a kind mother *within the laws of health;* but outside of those laws her stripes are so certain, so severe, and so relentless, that sometimes it seems almost as if the mother-kindness were turned to demon-malignity. So, in the field of morals, responsibility and power are coupled in a yoke that draws evenly and needs to gall but little; but when the power is *germinal,* and may produce an untamable creature, who may riot around the field and bellow hoarse defiance to all authority, Responsibility shrinks from *such* a yoke-fellow. Yet here, as in disease, system, law, authority reign. And if the parent trembles in view of the *dread* possibilities of the case, he may also rejoice in the sweep of the rich, beneficent and compensative possibilities that lie concealed in the holy word, "parent."

4. *Theoretical.*

1. "*The classification of sanctification* gives too much ground to self-exculpation."

Answer: God wants enlightened, not blinded, children; hence, if there be a basis in fact for the discriminations made, we need have no fear that our Science, made out of his facts, will harm his cause. Besides, if the objection has weight in this connection, it has the same against all enlightenment in matters of disease, wherefrom might be gathered excuses for inaction in the interests of health.

2. "In attributing depravity to the soul and body, the plain teachings of the Scriptures are denied, and a doctrine of the old Grecian philosophy is foisted into Christianity."

Answer: If our position be correct, it is none the worse for its Grecian paternity. If it really contradicts the Bible, one or the other must go down, and we may be very sure the Bible will not; but a seeming discrepancy only may not necessarily be fatal. Dewey (*"Problem of Human Destiny,"* pp. 92-97) argues strenuously in behalf of body purity, and throws the entire responsibility of perversion upon the mind. Such *seems* to be the doctrine of Matt. 15 : 19, 20, "Out of the heart proceed evil thoughts, murders, adulteries, fornications, theft, false witness, blasphemies; these are the things which defile man; but to eat with unwashed hands defileth not a man."

But we should remember that these sayings of the Savior were designed and understood (at least by the Pharisees) as an attack upon the Pharisaical doctrine of the supremacy of ceremonial observances. He did not even raise the question whether the moral defilement was resident in the body, soul, or spirit, but simply declared that the fruits of indwelling evil were defilement, while a non-observance of a mere ceremonial act was not defilement. True, he characterized these indwelling evils as "of the heart;" but when we call to mind the facts (as found upon a hasty examination, and not claimed to be *precisely* accurate) that six distinct Hebrew words and two Greek words are translated heart in our version, and that those six Hebrew words are translated also by at least nineteen other English words besides heart, and that the two Greek words occurring 120 times in the New Testament are used in twenty-two different senses, and that our English word heart has about twenty different meanings, few will be disposed to base a doctrine upon such an indeterminate expression.

Moreover, admitting all that we claim relative to the habit-perversions of soul and body, it is strictly true that, though murders, adulteries, etc., may be flesh-born, they must be will-adopted before they can appear in words and deeds, and therefore they always manifest heart-defilement. Hence we find no antagonism whatever between this passage and the statements of this treatise. Nor can we recall any passage which unequivocally declares that the seat of the "roots of bitterness"—"the carnal nature" still surviving in those who are in a justified state—is in the spirit or moral nature, as distinct from the soul and body.

3. "The asserted eradication of artificial appetites is all a delusion, since no man can be sure that the appetite supposed to be taken away, will not suddenly revive."

Answer: That there are physiological and, therefore, psychological difficulties in the doctrine, we will not deny. But, if we are under an economy of supernatural and, therefore, super-physiological grace, the difficulties do not concern us. The whole question is one of *fact*, to be determined by testimony under the ordinary rules of evidence. And here we hazard the opinion that no man who has carefully examined the evidence, dare to affirm either: (1) That the witnesses do not give clear, intelligible and uncontradictory statements of what they believe to be their own personal experience; or (2) That they are not as competent as ordinary men to understand their own experience; or (3) That they are not as truthful as ordinary men; or (4) That there are not thousands of them all testifying to the one point of eradication of artificial appetites by grace.

We demand, therefore, that their evidence shall be accepted, or that the objector shall exhibit his *authority* for discarding such evidence, merely because it does not coincide with his theories.

The supposition that the appetite may suddenly revive is altogether without weight, because many of the witnesses have lived many years after its extirpation, and *it has never revived.* If the subject were to fall into habitual sin, it is very probable that the law of association or the "residuum" of the old condition might again cause it to appear.

4. "The doctrine of 'faith-cures' belonged to the early church, passed away with it, has no foundation in *fact* in these times, and tends to fanaticism."

Answer: (1) Many testimonies are given in "these times" with a great degree of particularity of the *actual* and *successful* use of this early church privilege. See *"Dorothea Trudell;"* Dr. C. Cullis' *"Cures by Faith;" "My 25th Year Jubilee,"* by the author of this treatise (detailing his own cure after 25 years of lameness) and many other similar works.

(2) Many of these narrations cannot be impeached upon the ground of defect of piety, or intelligence, or special predisposition to, or habitual indulgence in, extreme and fanatical views on the part of their authors.

(3) The cures *are not denied.*

(4) But they are attributed by objectors to one or more natural causes, such as hopeful nervous excitement, imagination, etc.

(5) If they are such cures as this book advocates, they are wrought by Spirit-suggested and Spirit-helped faith.

(6) Such faith is a subjective mind and spirit exercise, in the very nature of the case known primarily, and perhaps only, to the mind concerned. The causation lies necessarily *beyond the view* of all others, and can be recognized only in the *consciousness* of the suppliant.

(7) But mere natural forces *can* and *do* in multitudes of cases produce the same results of physical healing.

(8) The real question in a genuine faith-cure is—*not* what *might* have done it, but—what actually DID it? It is a question of *fact*, not possibilities. If a man and a boy stand side by side, either of whom can throw a stone through a neighboring window, and a stone is actually thrown by the *man*, it is useless to say that the boy *could have done it*, or even that he *has been in the habit* of doing such things. *Did* he do it? That is the point, and the *only* point, to be settled.

(9) Just at this point, many good Christian men are guilty of a piece of *audacious assumption*, rivalled only by that of the most conscienceless skeptics of all the ages, in utterly *ignoring* in the subjects of cure, the CONSCIOUSNESS OF THEIR SPIRIT-HELPED FAITH.

(10) By the *same* process, and with *equal justice* and *right*, the skeptic may repudiate these objectors' *consciousness of personal salvation*, and attribute the external change wrought in their conversion, to policy, fear, or any other of the natural forces that is known to effect similar external revolutions in conduct, and they *are utterly powerless to reply;* for they have put the process into the the hands of the caviler, with the emphatic endorsement of their own example. During five years of patient waiting and careful watching, the writer has read everything that has fallen under his notice upon this question, and with especial interest all the replies to his own "25th Year Jubilee," and he will here record the fact for the astonishment of men, that *not one* has appeared that was not emptied of all logical and scientific value by this cardinal defect—*viz: Ignoring the consciousness of Spirit-helped faith.* We call upon objectors to rally to the assault of this one citadel of the faith-cure doctrine, and to conduct their approaches in such a way that atheists and infidels shall not be able to explode their own mines under their home-foundations, or else cease this endless endeavor to "steady the ark" of God, as if he were not able to care for his own cause.

(11) But the doctrine "tends to fanaticism,"

still responds the objector. If God's promises are anything more than meaningless tantalizations of human hope, their fulfillment will always and necessarily tend to fanaticism, if by that word is meant zealous and fearless proclamation of what God has done for personal deliverance. But if "wild and extravagant notions of religion" (Webster) are meant, then the answer and the denial are contained in the very condition of the *Spirit suggested and Spirit-helped prayer.*

5. "Sanctification is a work of grace, and cannot be supposed to produce any direct physical effects. Therefore, there can be no foundation for the hypothesis that brain and nerves are subject to spirit-influence as is stated on page 144."

Answer: The objection assumes too much. We know but little of the mysteries of life. The facts of *mesmerism* (now admitted by all men of science) are as far beyond explanation, and seem quite as unreasonable, as the supposition objected to. Again: Take the facts of human *Hibernation*, of which many unimpeachable examples are on record. One of the most celebrated of these is that of a fakir, " who was actually buried alive at Lahore, in 1837, in presence of Runjeet Sing and Sir Claude Wade, and who was dug up and restored to consciousness several months afterward, after every precaution had been taken to prevent anyone from disturbing the grave in the interval." A recent issue of the *Druggists' Circular* gave an extended account of the long and painful preparation, extending through years, through which the fakir passes before submitting to the hibernating state. After all it is only a little more marvelous than the forty-days' fast of Dr. Tanner.

Now, until men explain these wonders, we see no particular sagacity in denying that the Holy Spirit can touch physical sensibilities, affect nervous conditions, or even change brain-cells if need be. That he does affect physical sensations, is proven beyond a question.

From the *Life of Bishop Hamline*, by Dr. Hibbard, we take in his own words the following experience: "Suddenly I felt as if a hand omnipotent, not of wrath but of love, were laid upon my brow. That hand, as it pressed upon me, moved downward. It wrought within and without, and wherever it moved it seemed to leave the impress of the Savior's glorious image. For a few minutes the deep of God's love swallowed me up. All its billows rolled over me."

Dr. Daniel Steele's *Love Enthroned*, p. 280, says: "Suddenly I became conscious of a mysterious power exerting itself upon my sensibilities. My physical sensations, though not of a nervous temperament, in good health, sitting alone and calm, were like those of electric sparks passing through my bosom with slight but painless shocks, melting my hard heart into a fiery stream of love. Christ became so unspeakably precious that I instantly dropped all earthly good—reputation, property, friends, family, everything — in the twinkling of an eye, my soul crying out:

> 'None but Christ to me be given—
> None but Christ, in earth or heaven.'

He stood forth, as my Savior, all radiant in his loveliness, 'chiefest among ten thousand.' Yet there was no phantasm or image, or uttered word, apprehended by my intellect."

Such testimonies, from such sources, hush all cavil as to the facts alleged.

6. "Too much stress is laid upon the suggestions of the Holy Spirit in the absence of any adequate criteria by which to discriminate them from those of our own minds and those which come from Satan."

Answer: There are criteria by which the Spirit's suggestions may be known. His sheep "know his voice." (John 10 : 4.)

Spirits may know thought-voices as well as we do the voices of friends. His voice has certain characteristics, which can be apprehended and recognized by the sheep. These characteristics are:—

(1) There is no uncertainty in his utterances. His tones are never disguised either by accident or purpose. Friends sometimes imitate the tones of strangers or others in order to test the power of recognition of those whom they attempt to deceive. But his voice never assumes what belongs to another. It is always itself—pure and simple. Neither are his words ever equivocal. No double meaning can be attached to them. Nor are they ever mere sound without substance, or emptied of authoritative significance by weakness of expression. He never says, "*Perhaps* it would be well to do this or that, or to refrain from doing;" but always—*positively*, "Do!" or, "Do not!"

(2) If simulation or any other element of uncertainty (causing *honest* doubt) is present, his voice never requires recognition without giving time for investigation. Hence, great haste in a suggested duty, unless the voice be recognizable *at once* as his, is proof that the suggestion is not from him. He is not a hard master, demanding obedience in advance of rational conviction of obligation.

(3) His voice always issues from an open door of his providence; *i. e.*, where there is a real suggestion of present duty from him, there is always

an *opportunity* corresponding with the suggestion. His voice and providence work together. Hence, an urgency to go immediately in a way not open cannot spring from the impulses of the Spirit.

(4) His suggestions always correspond with the *principles* of the Word. Upon a certain occasion the writer positively promised a congregation that the meeting would be closed *immediately* after another short prayer. As soon as the prayer was concluded, a brother rushed across the platform and begged permission to exhort, which was promptly denied, very much to the chagrin of the brother, who was greatly offended, because "the Spirit commanded him to talk." But the writer could not see how or why the Holy Spirit should desire him to *falsify his word* before the congregation. Hence, he regarded the suggestion to exhort as proceeding from a " zeal not according to knowledge," rather than from the Spirit of all truth. So, if our duty absorbs all our energies at the moment, it cannot be our duty at the same moment to do anything else whatever; for the Scriptures enjoin us " to do with our might what our hands find to do."

Such are the characteristics of His voice, which, if carefully noted, and judiciously applied, will solve nearly all questions of duty. But there is another test—1 John 4 : 2—" *Hereby* know ye the Spirit of God: Every spirit that confesseth that Jesus Christ is come in the flesh is of God."

The *incarnation* was then the battle-ground between God and Satan. To accept that fact was to side with God. It is not so now. Satan himself admits that fact. Hence, some other test is now requisite. Here it is—1 Cor. 6 : 19, 20— " Ye are not your own : for ye are bought with a price ; therefore, glorify God in your body and in your spirit, which are God's." This is the substitute for the other, because it reiterates the fact of incarnation, gives its logical result—" Ye are not your own"—and lays down the consequent moral obligation : " Therefore, glorify God in your body and in your spirit, which are God's."

This *moral obligation* is *now* the battle-ground between God and Satan. Hence, any suggestion of duty that is in perfect accordance with this moral obligation, and at the same time has the *voice-qualities* that have been stated as belonging to Him, may be safely acted on at any time, and all results may be confidently left at his disposal. Beloved, " Try the spirits," whether they are of God.

7. " I can find nothing in the Bible about peculiar constitutions."

Answer : Very well. Does the objector find anything there that denies the fact that some men have peculiar constitutions? If not, its *silence* upon this point is no more evidence against that fact than its silence concerning multitudes of other facts universally admitted to be true, is evidence that they are not real. There are some things that do not need to be revealed, and so general are the provisions of grace that there may be no call for special recognition even; yet they may have an important place in a systematic presentation of closely related truths.

8. "There are remnants of the old depravity existing after regeneration."

Answer: By this we understand is meant, within the spirit of the regenerated person; for if it be affirmed of the soul and body, the objection in nowise differs from the views herein set forth. A. Nash, in "*Full Salvation,*" p. 18, says: "A complete revelation of depravity in penitence would drive into hopeless despair." On the other hand, Crane, in "*Holiness the Birth-right of All God's Children,*" pp. 69–70, says: "If there is a single passage of Scripture which directly asserts that one born of God, and in a normal condition as a regenerated soul, still has a degree of depravity in him, where is that passage? It is really surprising that a doctrine should go so long unquestioned, when its ablest adherents show so scanty an array of Scripture, and prove so little by it.

Wesley, in his sermon on 'Sin in Believers,' cites but six passages to prove the doctrine, and not one of them clearly contains it." He then reviews the passages with the following results: (1) Gal. 5 : 17—spoken to a backslidden church, and not applicable to all genuine Christians. (2) 1 Cor. 3 : 1, 3, 4—written to those in the particular conditions named, and not applicable to others in a better condition. (3) 2 Cor. 7 : 1—simply a strong appeal to continue in the love of God, not in any sense a confession. (4) (5) (6) The Spirit's address to the churches of Ephesus, Pergamos and Sardis. All these were to those who "had left their first works," hence could not be descriptive of those who had *not* done so. We are quite willing to leave the objection where Dr. Crane has, certainly until his trenchant argument is answered.

PART III.—THE EXPERIENCE.

Having in Part I. outlined the Philosophy of Christian Holiness, and in Part II. stated the Theory, perhaps too concisely, we now proceed to the more congenial, and we trust more profitable, consideration of its Experience. We are fully aware of the points of divergence of this from other works upon the great theme, and are quite alive to the danger of erroneous deductions from positions so briefly stated, and sometimes apparently so overdrawn. But the reader should be reminded that in a work of this kind subjects that are made prominent by all writers upon the theme, may be stated here without the *lengthy treatment* that other points which have been generally passed by absolutely require in order to receive the attention they deserve. E. g., The agency of the Holy Spirit—all-important as it is—is allotted less space than the physiological and hereditary aspects of the subject. Were this book designed as an exact systematic presentation of the theme, this disparity would be an imperfection; but, in reality, this treatise is largely *supplemental*. It is a philosophy—very brief, but, it is believed, lacking in no element of a true philosophy. It is a theory—dangerously concise, yet containing all the elements of a correct theory. It is an experience in the sense of being a condensation and transcription of multitudes of recorded experiences, modified by those other phases of experience which have not been so frequently recorded, in the hope that some may be thereby aided to a better life, and others equally helped to more charitable views, and more encouraging expressions.

CHAPTER I.

PRACTICAL DEDUCTIONS.

1. *Explanatory of the way.*

In view of the general demands of Christian consistency, it should now be assumed that the reader who has patiently plodded through the two preceding parts of this work, is ready to go forward from this point *as a seeker*, if not already in the possession of the grace. His prayerful attention is therefore invited to the following statements:

1. It is a way of positive *self-assertion*. "Consciousness of the validity of our efforts," is stated on page 72 as a *principle;* and "The testimony of each faculty unimpeachable within its appro-

priate sphere," is declared on page 77 as a *law*. In these respects, therefore, the seeker must believe in, and rely upon the trustworthiness of self with no degree of hesitation or wavering. For just in the ratio of his doubt or indecision here will be faltering and failure in the attainment of his object. Satan asks no better field in which to scatter his temptations than amid the endless perplexities engendered by a want of this kind of self-assertion.

The humility that starts back alarmed at this statement, and shudders at self-reliance in all its forms, is a false or misguided lowliness. If we cannot trust our consciousness of honest effort to do our part, we cannot trust His promises, because we can have no assurance that we have complied with their conditions.

If we cannot rely upon our will to make a full and immediate surrender, we can never know but we are still rebels in purpose and in fact. Hence, we must stand firmly and immovably upon the basis of a positive self-assertion in order to reach upward to the higher standpoint of sanctified transformation.

2. But it is also a way of the highest *self-abnegation*. Recalling the normal laws of spiritual life as stated upon page 85, a glance will satisfy the most incredulous that the seeming opposites,

viz., self-abnegation and self-assertion, can and must co-exist in the experience of the mature Christian; self-assertion so far as it is necessarily implied in a conditional and confident faith, and self-abnegation as to acceptance of God's Christ and God's will.

Yet, it is not a self-abnegation of the mystical sort that avows an utter "deadness" of the sensibilities to the impulses of the flesh and the enticements of sin. If such a state be attainable, and probably it is, it is an undesirable absorption which can never be of practical benefit to the world.

Concerning our first parents, Caldwell, "*Philosophy of Christian Perfection,*" p. 22, says: "Their natural sensibilities were susceptible of being addressed and excited, in view of even forbidden and unlawful objects: and this excitement might *innocently* amount even to a *conscious tendency to seek their gratification in such forbidden objects*... This alone can give temptation its effect, and call forth the power of moral resistance." We cannot hope to reach a better state in this life than that which they enjoyed.

The self-abnegation which we insist upon in this connection is rather the emptying out and casting away of all the claims of self that come into competition with, or antagonize the claims of God, while clinging with even stronger tenacity to those which may be yoked into his service.

3. Such self-abnegation necessarily implies *entire consecration, i. e., complete* devotement to do the will of Him in whose favor self is denied. It may be an *act*, as when some specific revelation of God's will arouses the antagonism of self, and necessitates such a particular devotement, or it may be a *state* wherein a preponderating self-abnegation settles beforehand all such antagonisms by a pre-ordained and pre-disposed submission— " that state of devotedness to God and his service required by the moral law." (Prof. Finney.) " A supreme reference to the will of God and glory of God in all things; using and enjoying all as he wills we should; disclaiming any rights that conflict with his rights; pursuing such business, and in such manner as from our best light we believe is according to the will of God; using all the proceeds of our labor precisely as we believe God directs; loving those objects, and in that degree, which he approves; doing those acts which will be for his glory; living in the world, but living for God:—whoever does this consecrates himself to God." (Foster, " *Christian Purity*," p. 205.)

Such a consecration has no looking after reserve rights, no haggling after easier terms, no bargaining for future restoration of abandoned possessions, no seeking after special exemptions, but is just a fee-simple transfer of rights, interests, claims, *everything*, to the sovereignty of God.

4. It is a way of *invincible resolution*. No feeble purpose, no faltering will, can hold to this high-way. Stimulated by the intense desires that are quickened into power by the convictions of so grand a privilege and so imperative a necessity, the Will must survey all difficulties with unblanching cheek and untrembling nerve, and march steadily forward to grasp a prize that will be yielded to no vacillating resolution. To find or die, to attain or perish! is the battle-cry that must be hurled into the teeth of all oppositions, and must thrill with new inspirations every despondent moment, and every relaxing energy.

Spirit-hunger that *will* find food; heart-throbbings that yearn to be hushed to rest; soul-tempests that *must* surcease their wailings; finite graspings that clutch and hold the Infinite—all these focalized in one imperious, commanding, changeless *Resolve*, swaying a present scepter of absolute dominion over the nature, and projecting itself along the currents of life that flow into the future—such must be the determination with which the seeker for purity prosecutes his search.

Anything short of this is compromise in advance—almost surrender upon call.

Let the reader stop just here, and ask the serious question : Have *I* the self-assertion, self-abnegation, consecration, and resolution which this great experience demands? With introspective vision, let the heart-searching which this question implies, be deeply, thoroughly, persistently made. Let no surface work suffice. Let no voice of postponement be heeded. Now, here, in the presence of an unmeasured possibility of good, search the foundations, that you may build and build speedily upon the unyielding Rock.

5. It is also a way of *unquestioning faith.* Whether or not the suggestion from science be accepted, and the Holy Spirit be deemed to touch the periphery of the ideational nerves (pp. 50–51) with a Divine influence that goes down through the nature—thrilling thoughts, affections, will, and even sensations—it is most certainly to be assumed by the seeker that *somewhere* and *somehow* the Mighty Transformer can so touch the depravities of the *my* that the belongings of the spirit shall be rendered accordant with His will. O, what a touch is that! So marvelously moulding — so transcendantly transforming! Holy Spirit, bring it to the reader's heart!

But such gifts of God are not cast like sun-beams on the world, whether the world be willing or not to feel their glow. They belong to the higher realm of free gifts upon conditions named.

The one condition comprehensive of all others, upon which the *touch of God* is suspended, is, UNQUESTIONING FAITH. But what is that? Let not the anxious reader expect an answer in a single sentence. Heart-work embraces much. To make haste we must move slowly until we are in the beaten way. The elements of this *condition-faith* are the following:

(1) A clear conviction that God has promised cleansing to *me*. No matter how strong may be my assurance that he has promised it to others, that will not suffice. *I* am the important factor in this problem. If to *me* he has pledged his sanctifying grace it is well; but if to all others and not to me, I am nothing better. Just here assurance must be explicit and decisive. Not the shadow of a doubt may becloud it.

Has the reader such a conviction? If so, the way is prepared to move forward to another step.

(2) The clear conviction that God's promise is conditional upon my performance of certain things, all of which I may *know*, and concerning which I may be *positively sure* whether I comply or not, and just *when* I comply if I do at all.

A conviction as comprehensive as this should

not be passed over without a second or even third reading. The word "conditioned" contains the very germ of all possibilities in this direction. He does give sanctifying grace to some. He does *not* give it to others. Since he "is no respecter of persons"—why? Because it is not a free gift, but a *conditioned* gift—*i. e.*, a consequence dependent upon certain things that we may do or not, just as we choose, and if we do them the consequence will ensue, but if we refuse to do them it will not occur.

Now, my conviction of the conditionality of this grace must be as clear and positive as my existing conviction that God has promised it to *me*. No hint even of any exception whatever may be harmlessly entertained for a moment. It may be had, but it can only be found in exact compliance with certain prescribed conditions.

Further, these conditions I may *know*. Conditions that may not be known are not *conditions* in the religious sense. They may be excuses for a tyrant, or reasons for a knave, but conditions they cannot be, because an elemental idea of such a condition is—*a contingency within the will of one, upon which contingency the actions of another are dependent.* To suppose such contingency to be unknown to the first as a condition, is to suppose him to be within the realm of chance and not within that of free and responsible activity. Hence, that I may know the conditions is a conclusion that must be as strongly affirmed and as resolutely adhered to as any fact bearing upon this subject.

Still, further, knowing the conditions I may be certain whether I comply with them or not. To doubt on this point would be to question the truthfulness of our own consciousness, and by so doing *utterly invalidate all knowledge.* By the same testimony I may know just *when* I comply, for consciousness has no memory and no anticipation. It is an on-living *now:* a seeing within as interior facts transpire.

Having these three convictions, *viz.*, knowledge of conditions, compliance, and time when, rooted deeply in the mind, then comes—

(3) Undoubting confidence that just so soon as the conditions are complied with, God will *immediately* accomplish his part of the work, according to the principle laid down on page 67. No interval can be allowed for any reason whatever, because any supposable reason would thereby be deemed to be *stronger than his infinite repulsions against sin.* And if it could prevail to withhold the cleansing for one moment, it might for an hour, a day, a year, a life-time! Such a conclusion cannot be admitted; therefore God's imme-

diate cleansing operation—upon the removal of the barriers—must be assumed so confidently that our consciousness of compliance with the conditions shall be the premise of a faith-logic, with a *therefore* as clear as a sunbeam and as decisive as fact; and that "therefore" must begin the assertion—"*He cleanseth me now.*"

(4) Then comes a *desire* for the blessing sufficiently strong to induce the compliance demanded. In some natures so sensitively adjusted to the right that to see duty is to begin its performance, a very small degree of special desire may be sufficient, because of the imperiousness of conscience. But in most cases the will needs the reinforcement of strong desire, and sometimes of vehement emotion even, to enable it to comply with the conditions required. Hence, if the seeker still hesitates, and perhaps wonders why he does not take the decisive step, it may be well for him to feed his desires for purity by appropriate meditations, and by prayer for hunger; also by much devout reading of God's Word and of the biographies of those who have enjoyed the grace. By these means he will most certainly find kindled within him an intense longing that will give to the moral nature all the stimulus that emotion is designed to impart, and thus, with all his reserve power brought to the front, he will be able

to "make the venture" from which he has shrunk so long.

(5) Actual, conscious, present, complete compliance, (according to the conviction named as the second element of this condition-faith,) *as a specific act*, for this particular end, is now needful. Coming up to this point in the use of even a large degree of consecration, and then waiting in a haze of dreamy semi-expectancy for "the fire to descend and consume the sacrifice," will not prove successful. Purity is clearness as well as cleanness. Mists and fogs may sometimes mar clearness of vision in other things, but here the atmosphere *must* be transparent. The validity of present observations, and the reliability of future calculations, will be largely affected by it. Hence, he who would move surely in this "highway" must see clearly every step of the progress into it, and especially the one that he is about to make.

A certain specified compliance is demanded as an inexorable condition. Do I comply, or do I not? If I do *not*, the matter is settled beyond a doubt, I *cannot* have the blessing. If I do comply, the matter is settled as conclusively as in the other case, but in the opposite way—I *can* have the blessing.

If I do not know whether I comply or not, again the matter is settled *adversely*, for *no posi-*

tive faith can ground itself upon a negative! The faith that claims this coveted experience is a very positive one, and an equally explicit one. It does not deal in glittering generalities, nor rest upon "hope so" or "suppose so," but upon the calm, deliberate immovable *know so; i. e.*, upon the knowledge of present, complete, compliance with the conditions named.

(6) Then comes the *consequent assumption* that inasmuch as I have certainly complied with the conditions, I now rest entirely and exclusively upon the *veracity of God*, and THEREFORE do NOW RECEIVE within myself his sanctifying grace. As an intellectual act this assumption does not rest upon any *sensible* change, nor upon any *perceived difference* in the state of the heart, but solely upon two facts: First, That God has promised it immediately upon certain conditions. Second, That I do now fulfill those conditions.

What then? Joy may instantly spring up. A conscious change may at once supervene. Peace *must* be abiding. The witness of the Holy Spirit may be instantaneous. But if none of these except the peace be present, the seeker has simply to remain in the attitude of assumption here described, until it shall please God to add the witness, which certainly will come, and very likely in an unlooked-for moment.

At this point the reader should beware of the common tendency to look back into the heart to see if any change justifies the belief in present cleansing. That is to go by sight, not by faith; but we are saved by faith, and the seeker has nothing to do with his heart, but simply to leave it in God's hands, while he believes.

6. It is now a way of *immovable trust.* Says Rev. W. H. M. Aitken in the " *The School of Grace :*"

"I read in a friend's book, not long ago, an extract which commenced with the following words: 'The longer I live the more profoundly am I convinced that the all-in-all of practical Christianity may be summed up in two words— submit and commit.' Truer words have seldom passed from human pen; and this is the great lesson that grace by her gentle discipline teaches, and that the will of man has to learn. Submit, cease first from thy rebellious self-assertions, and next from thy proud efforts to correct and amend thyself; and then commit—cast thyself into the hands of Omnipotent Love. Claim it of the new Adam that he shall, dwelling within thee, accomplish, as he has undertaken, what thou canst not do, and regulate in peace and harmony, under his scepter, the once jarring and conflicting forces of thy nature. So shall there indeed be a great calm, a stillness, a rest within thy consecrated heart, and thou shalt be in a position to make proof of all the wealth of thy promised land—

the land that flows with milk and honey—as thou proceedest to live, not only soberly, but righteously and godly. Only let us take heed lest it should be said of thee or of me, reader, 'We see that they could not enter in, because of unbelief.'"

This trust is the state of committal here described. It is a steady holding of self in the position gained. There may be bending before the sweep of the flood, as the rush bends in the swollen stream, but it is only that it may hold the better by the rootlets that penetrate beneath the flow. So, blasts of temptation may rush with almost irresistible power over the spirit, and to outward seeming it may be prostrated by their fury; but down deep amid the foundation purposes of being, one master-purpose may link it in unvarying consciousness to its anchorage in God, and when the storm is overpast, it will rise straight and strong as though it had never bowed to the tempest that strove to uproot it. There may be a cry of human sorrow that asks for light, and that light may be denied; yet when sight fails, and reason falters, and love itself almost questions, there will be a persistence in trust that will defy all blindness and weakness, and will go on clinging amid all storms and tempests, simply because its only business is to cling. When once the conviction thoroughly permeates the nature that God does all the work of cleansing and keeping clean — the first upon the conditions named at length, and the second upon the further condition of our abiding trust—it is easy to comprehend that *trust is the business of our lives.*

7. It is a way of determined and systematic *avoidance of the abnormal.* It will be well for the reader just at this point to return to page 88 and searchingly inquire, " Is my acceptance of Christ complete, in the sense of measuring up to my needs ?" If this can be answered in the affirmative, then passing to page 89, let the touchstone of submission to God's will be applied; and if no rebellion be found, then let present consecration be compared with the demands of God's work; and if it be not defective, and if no self-guidance or self-dependence mar the symmetry of Christian development, (page 90,) the conclusion may be reached that there is no criminal "neglect of the proffered aid of the Holy Spirit," and no spiritual abnormality now resident within. Now the safeguards of determined and systematic avoidance must be reared. Determination there must have been already, else the present experience would not have been acquired. But system is needed as well. The outposts must be manned. Sentries must stand guard. Surprise must be prevented. Assault must be rendered

fruitless. And when the march is commanded, ambush must be guarded against. All this means tireless watchfulness against the evils that no longer hold the citadel of the heart, and the exercise of common sense in avoiding special exposures to them.

But, while the reader who has thus carefully searched his foundations may be duly grateful for the grace given, there are certain mental abnormalities that should receive attention.

Mental instability and excessive mental bias (pages 90–91) have been named; and should there exist any appreciable degree of either in the constitution, it should be disciplined with the utmost promptness and the greatest decision that can be summoned to the work. A candid revelation of the weakness to a judicious friend might be of great service. But prayer, watchfulness, and a careful *development of the opposite traits of character* must be the chief dependence, and these must never be remitted for a day until the evil is corrected.

Besides all this, there are Laws of abnormal mental development and action, specified as Perversity, pages 78–82, Irregularity, page 82, and Distrust, page 84. These should be very carefully scanned to see if there be danger lurking there. If the reader be unfortunately afflicted with the temperamental perversity, his wisdom will consist in scrupulously avoiding temptation and all those causes of wrong impulses which experience has proved to be detrimental, or which Reason declares from the nature of the case must be so. If, after all this care, the impulses sometimes or perhaps frequently sweep the nature beyond the moorings of prudence despite the resistance of the regulative faculties and grace, and notwithstanding a persistent consciousness of *doing his best*, then must the reader, with whatever sorrow of heart it may come, accept the sad conviction that he is blighted out of the ranks of normal humanity by some curse of heredity, and thereby consigned to the specific type whose highest sanctification has been described upon pp. 127-9, 148.

But it is not probable, if it be possible even, that one who has passed unscathed through the searching ordeal of introspection here assumed, should be thus perverted. His danger is far more likely to be irregularity—the habitual disuse, or excessive use of certain faculties. We cannot more clearly indicate what this is than by emphatically urging the reader to peruse with care what is said upon this point on pp. 83, 84. In this whole treatise we have studiously avoided useless amplification, but our sense of the practical importance of this subject is a strong inducement to go at length into details just here. But let this hint suffice to awaken the reader to a keen sense of imminent spiritual danger, if in his case *each faculty does not do its own work and that only.*

If the full significance of this caution be now apprehended, let us add one more, viz.: Beware of the law of Distrust! Page 84 tells *why;* and he who would live this "higher life" must avoid all abnormal conditions of mind and spirit as he values success in his efforts. But can it be supposed that this obligation stops with the mental and spiritual? The laws of abnormal physical development and action have been laid down on pages 93–6, and so far as they are avoidable, there can be no question that he who would live purely before God must scrupulously abstain from all acts, and especially from all habits that would bring him under the dominion of those laws.

Simple disturbance of function (p. 94) according to the organ implicated and the extent of the disturbance, may exhibit all the thought-changes depicted in "The Confessions of an Opium Eater," that is, from the uttermost depths of self-abhorrence and despair to the topmost heights of phrenzied ecstacy, with no change whatever in external or moral relations. If it be assumed that this may be innocently done with no higher motive than self-gratification, then it follows that practical lunacy may be occasioned at pleasure with no violation of Christian obligations, which is the same as to say that such obligations may be obliterated with no violence to them, which is furthermore to affirm that there are no Christian obligations.

If, then, temporary lunacy may not be innocently induced for the purpose of self-gratification, neither can any other derangement of function that to any extent affects thought unfavorably, be voluntarily produced without transgression of the laws of Christian life. The same course of argument holds good in reference to "Organic change of functional products" (p. 95) and organic change of tissues (p. 95).

Man is not his own master. And if he were, his surrender to God in conversion leaves him with no reserve rights. As a Christian he belongs to God. His mission is to glorify God. But professed reverence for God's written law, conjoined with known and purposed and habitual violation of his other laws, is at best a mixed and semi-rebellious service which can never meet the high demands of his rights and the interests of his kingdom.

Let no one, therefore, who strives to walk in

the "high-way of holiness," pollute it with indulgences that the laws of health and nature condemn. And if he does, let him not lay the flattering unction to his soul, that God loves his profession more than he does the laws that he has established "for a thousand generations." No! His will is *his*, whether it be written on tables of stone, spoken upon Galilean hills, crystalized in marble strata, woven in tissues of nerve and flesh, sphered in worlds or tear-drops, mantled in evening's glow or maiden's blush, voiced in the harmonies of the spheres or the praises of his children! *His laws are his own*, and are not to be tampered with to suit the convenience or the perversions of self-seeking mortals.

Obedience is honor to him! Unvarying deference is his glory. Determined and systematic avoidance of the abnormal is therefore a duty incumbent upon every one who would preserve "a conscience void of offence" and illustrate the glorious declaration of the apostle: "As he is, so are we in this world."

2. *Advisory as to methods.*

1. Make right discriminations as to what is required. There is no more frequent hindrance than mistakes as to the nature and extent of the obligations attending this life of faith. (See Fletcher's *Treatise on Christian Perfection*, 32mo.

page 34.) Nor are these errors confined to the unintelligent or uncultured, for we often find them held by the most intellectual, educated and conscientious believers. Hence, right discriminations at the outset may save from many a quicksand on the journey. And if some of these distinctions seem absurd and uncalled for, to some of our readers, they should remember that the human mind is the breeding-place of all manner of strange and foolish phantasies, and that the experience of the new birth gives no exemption in this respect; therefore, if the critic be fortunately placed upon the high grounds of clear and extended views, he should pity the less favored who dwell amid the murky fogs which distort the objects of their vision, and rejoice at any effort for their good.

(1) An exact correspondence of real with ideal Christian life is not to be expected. The ideal is the product of the imaginative faculty working under the stimulus of an active (possibly *over-active*) conscience, and building up the materials of intellectual conceptions into character-forms. It is therefore *purely artistic,* and like all other forms of art ought to *aim at perfection.* Just as the Greek painter who, when required to paint the most beautiful female possible, caused to be brought to his studio a number of the most fault-

less forms in the city, and selecting a hand of one, the bust of another, an eye of a third, the nose of a fourth, and so on, he combined these separate perfections into one figure that has been the marvel of the ages; so, the Christian selects the meekness of Moses, the faith of Elijah, the zeal of Paul, the love of John, and all other excellences of other saints, and embodying them all in one, holds that group of perfections before himself as that to which he is to aspire—his *ideal*. Real Christian life, on the other hand, is the work of affections and will prosecuted amid all the perversities of depravity, and all the oppositions of " the world, the flesh, and the devil."

It would be most singular, therefore, if the creative faculty of the imagination should not develop a type of character that the will and the affections thus burdened, would of necessity fail to realize in a corresponding experience. What then should be done? Certainly *not wear out life in hopeless efforts to reach the impracticable!* If the ideal be not perfect at the outset, the very attempt to reach it exalts it, and the nearer it be approximated the further it verges toward faultlessness. Hence it ever eludes the grasp of experience.

But there is one department of our being wherein there may be exact correspondence between the ideal and the real, viz., *the intentions.* We *can* intend to copy all the graces of all the saints just as far as the materials given to our hands permit the reproduction, so that if there be failure it shall not be chargeable to our want of right purpose. But when the inevitable failure occurs, it must be set down upon the ledger of our responsibility debited to constitutional infirmities, which, in a right state of the intentions, are covered by the blood of atonement. Let the desired correspondence, therefore, between the ideal and the real be confined to the intentions, and all will be well.

(2) A continued conscious environment of Deity, " *keeping*" the soul is not to be looked for. "If I do not sin, it is as good for me as if I were environed by the jasper walls and *could* not sin." —J. S. Inskip. These words point to a most important truth, viz., That the fact of sinlessness (in the Christian, not in the legal sense) is the test of goodness. If, then, we are kept from sin, the consciousness of the environing Deity is of little consequence, and its absence should occasion no disturbance whatever.

(3) A constant stretch of spirit after the higher, is not to be coveted.

Wings must sometimes rest or droop and fail. Their soaring capacity and upward instinct ought never to cease, but the loftiest flights, especially in the fury of the storm, antedate the sterner necessity for transient repose. The time may come when the spirit's soarings will be undisturbed by earthward calls, but now the body fetters, in (undesired it may be, but during life,) indissoluable bonds of weakness every aspiring spirit, and the constant stretch is synonomous with a speedy break. Indeed, it is a fact well known to the physician, that a brain suffering for better nutrition—a better supply of arterial blood—often stimulates to a zealous life where the " religious fervor is the measure of the cravings of the ungratified physiological aspirations.". (Fothergill, "Mental Aspects of Ordinary Disease," in Journal of Mental Science.)

Such being the case, we can well afford to attach but minor importance to the *uninterrupted* struggles of the spirit to reach loftier attainments, and content ourselves with such measure of active desire as will comport with healthful rest and sustained persistence of purpose.

The apparent necessity of continual wrestling of desire, is in reality but another phase of the disposition, so common to beginners especially, to find satisfaction, if not assurance, in emotional states.

(4) Complete control of the thoughts is not

to be hoped for. Scarcely any point in the whole range of Christian holiness is of greater practical importance than this. So many write such bitter things against themselves because of "wandering thoughts," and such multitudes are engaged in a desperate, though really utterly hopeless struggle to "control" their thoughts, that any discrimination that will self-sweeten the first and give some rest to the others will be a boon to be hailed with joy. First then, let it be carefully noted that thoughts are to a very great extent automatic, *i. e.*, They are the product of mechanism, and take their characteristics from their source. Now, lest the cry of materialism alarm the reader, let us hold in view certain facts, viz. :—

((1)) "Sir Francis Beaufort (*Brodie: Mind and Matter*, p. 135,) when preserved from drowning had " every incident of his former life glance across his recollection in retrograde succession, not in mere outline, but the picture being filled with every minute and collateral feature, forming a kind of panoramic view of his entire existence, each act of it accompanied by a sense of right and wrong."

A schoolmate of our own boyhood had a similar experience, and a policeman—a parishioner of the writer—affirmed that when he was shot in the cheek-bone in attempting to arrest a criminal, he had instantly a perfect panorama of his entire life. Other cases might be quoted, but these are sufficient to show that in certain states of the brain thoughts arise independently of the will.

We grant that these cases are extreme; *i. e.*, the stimulating cause in each was all that the system could endure; but the *effects* were extreme likewise. It is, therefore, reasonable to conclude that a minor cause may produce a less effect, so that a quantitative relation between a congested brain and its product—involuntary thought—will be found to subsist through all gradations of cerebral stimulation (unless carried to the point of exhaustion or coma), and will often be of sufficient magnitude to be of importance in this connection.

((2.)) Ordinary diseases, in many cases, have certain specific mental effects, *e. g.*, a slight amount of bile in the blood, or an excess of renal products, "may depress a man with hopeless despair or drive him into paroxysms of violent passion." ("*Dr. Fothergill, Popular Science Monthly,*" No. 35, p. 563.)

"It seems even, that bodily pain and disease are not only compatible with, but may directly contribute to, the loftiest efforts of the intellect. They sometimes positively enhance its powers. The effect of some disorders and of certain sorts of pain upon the nerves is to produce a cerebral excitation; and the stimulus thus communicated to the material organ of thought renders it for the time capable of unusual effort. . . . The wonderful eloquence of Robert Hall was doubtless greatly owing to the stimulating influence of a terrible spinal malady. Dr. Conolly mentions a gentleman whose mental faculties never reached their full power except under the irritation of a blister," W. R. Greg.—" *The Enigmas of Life.*"

The writer has observed in his own case that whenever he has been called to preach while suffering from a certain abdominal weakness to which he has been frequently subject, the efforts have almost invariably been characterized by a brilliancy and spirituality that have caused it to be matter of remark among the people, " Our pastor preaches best when he is sick."

" The mental attitude of sufferers from heart disease is usually one of caprice - unsustained volition ; together with suspiciousness and groundless fear,—imperfect emotional products." " The resultant product in gout is a blended compound of irritability and suspicion, bad temper and anxiety, the latter all the more aggravating from a consciousness that it is not mere illusion, but an emotional hallucination. Such individuals are the terror of their dependants. . . . There is such a villainous state of temper, at times ascending to ferocity, that the person becomes simply intolerable; the unfortunate sufferers themselves being still further tortured by the haunting impression that they are utterly unreasonable and that their attitude does not arise from any provocation from without, but that it takes its origin in some abnormal condition existing within." (Shown by Dr. Garrod to be excess of lithic acid in the blood.) "In one case well known to me the sufferer sought relief in religious exercises, in resort to her Bible and to prayer—it is needless to say without the desired result. . . . Well directed treatment produced a restoration of the normal feelings which all the spiritual exercises had failed to achieve." The mental attitude assumed in cancer is "that of sullen and defiant submission to the inevitable;" . . . while in pyæmia (alteration of the blood by pus) "from the first long shivering fit which marks the initiation of the fateful disease, the mental attitude is usually that of imperturable indifference."—*Fothergill.*

It is well known that in diseases of the lungs an utterly irrational hopefulness characterizes the progress of the sufferer down to the very gates of the grave, while in certain abdominal affections a depression that defies all hopefulness is equally marked.

The physiological explanation is — that the abdominal diseases cause a depletion of the emotional nerve centres, while the lung affections are attended with a plethoric condition of those centres, and the corresponding depression and exaltation are mental symptoms of these physical conditions. It is an admitted fact that heightened blood-pressure within the brain intensifies mental activity, and that excess of nitrogen in the blood tends to explosive irritability.

Two very singular cases of religious interest occasioned by cerebral disturbance came under the notice of the writer. The first was that of an apparently remarkably healthy wife and mother, who had been brought up religiously, but had not previously manifested special interest in the subject. Having been sent for, we found her deeply interested, accusing herself of great wickedness, and tortured with the continual obtrusion of thoughts too bad to be described.

After suitable instruction and prayer she became perfectly calm and trustful, in the consciousness of forgiveness. Calling the day after we found her still trustful, but tossed with tides of evil thoughts that seemed to *fill* her being. We at once commenced a searching investigation, and found that her life had not been such as to give the material for such thoughts: therefore they were not called up by association That no effort of will, and no exercise of prayer relieved her, more than momentarily; hence, the thoughts could not be the suggestions of Satan. A physical source seemed therefore most probable, and upon inquiry, she admitted that she had constant headache, unusual nervousness and almost utter sleeplessness. We at once advised her to abandon her case entirely to God, seek mental diversion in any practicable way, sleep at any cost, and send immediately for her physician. Within two weeks she was entirely prostrated, and at the request of the physician we saw her again, and found the mental symptoms seriously aggravated, and soon after she died. Did the religious interest cause, or was it the consequence of the brain-disease? So far as her safety is concerned it does not matter. She exercised intelligent faith in Christ, and such faith saves, *no matter how it may be induced.* Her interest commenced when she was entirely alone, far removed from any religiously exciting cause.

It was not violent enough to induce disease in so short a time.

The faculties involuntarily exercised were consciousness, imagination and conscientiousness, to which will and veneration stood opposed in ceaseless struggles, which would not have been the case had the origin of the trouble been religious excitement. Therefore, the Christian experience was undoubtedly the result of cerebral excitement; genuine nevertheless.

The second case was that of an intelligent gentleman who had carefully schooled himself in skeptical notions, but who came to some revival services of an undemonstrative kind that the writer was holding in his own church. When the invitation was given for penitents to come to the altar for prayer, this gentleman deliberately arose in the middle aisle, laid off his overcoat, and walked to the altar. Soon the meeting concluded and a moment's conversation convinced us that something was wrong. Not from anything that was said or done, but by the expression of his eye. The next eve, he arose as before, came entirely around and *within* the altar and in a few concise and telling words declared his acceptance of Christ as his Savior. Within twenty-four hours he was a raving maniac. A few weeks treatment at the asylum, however, completely restored him, and nearly five years of consistent Christian life have attested the reality of the change.

Jones, "*Man Moral and Physical*," p. 155, narrates the case of a New England preacher who arose to deliver his sermon, and instead announced that he had backslidden. Two weeks treatment restored him. And pp. 215-17, he details the case of an anxious mother, sleepless, fevered and agonizing, caring for nothing but the salvation of her children. Her physician wisely deemed the cause to be increased arterial action, and a few doses of tartar emetic restored her to a normal state.

Dr. D. Uwins, referred to on page 54, claimed to be able to direct the current of thought as he pleased in his insane patients by the use of narcotics. Anæsthetics, such as ether and chloroform, destroy consciousness and depress sensibility, but leave movements free. Curare destroys the power of movement but leaves sensibility and will unimpaired. Alcohol and opium in small doses exalt mental action. Belladonna and Indian hemp pervert mental action, even to artificial delirium. The spondylium heraclium of Kamtschatka impels to suicide. Nitrous oxide stimulates to most intense action, usually with visions of beauty, while carbonic acid gas stupifies into coma and death.

We once knew a very profane man who was subject to frequent fits of intoxication, each ending in helpless stupor : but at a certain stage he rarely failed to mount a cart, stone wall or other elevation and preach to his associates, delivering addresses full of religious sentiment and apparently of appropriate feeling.

Intermittent mania occurs with the same regularity and is cured by the same treatment as ague.

It is stated as a fact that the miasmata of the Niger, so fatal to Europeans, stimulates the worst passions of the natives; also that the north wind at Buenos Ayres spoils meat, milk and bread, and produces headache; and Jones, page 313, gives an account of an amiable gentleman who always quarreled with any one he met during the prevalence of that wind, and was finally executed for murder after twenty street fights with knives. The devoted Dr. Alexander of New Jersey, said: "It is merciless in Satan to assail me when the wind is east." When asked if he always enjoyed full assurance of faith, he answered, "Yes, except when the east wind blows."

Dr. Burrows tells of an eminent divine who was always maniacal except when he had pains in his spine. These illustrations of mind-conditionating force (see pages 35 and 53) we have thrown together in order to show that thought products depend upon the condition of the material organ of thought, therefore *when it is affected by disease or irritated by poisons in blood or atmosphere its functional results may be correspondingly modified.* Hence, it is vain to expect that the experience of Christian purity will so change the laws of our being that we shall be entitled to claim the entire control of our thoughts.

Is there, then, any criteria by which we may distinguish thoughts that are born of such bodily conditions from those which are voluntary? Darwin " *Zoonomia*, vol. 1, p. 184 says the latter " are always employed about the *means* to acquire pleasurable objects or to avoid painful ones; while the former are employed about the *possession* of those that are already in our power," *i. e.* voluntary thoughts are characterized by *judgment*, while those which spring from sensations (conscious or unconscious, either,) are marked by their paramount *impulsiveness*. Strange if this noted scientist has unwittingly furnished a key to a very large and important class of embarrassments in Christian life! Yet, with sufficient explanations, we think that he has made a suggestion of great value. Using his word, "acquire," in the sense of perpetuity of present "pleasurable objects," as well as in the sense of securing others; and giving to his word "avoid" the sense of riddance of present "painful objects," as well as eluding others not present;—and understanding his word "sensations" to be used as synonymous with Fenchtersleben's "innate sensation," (*Med. Psychology*, 1874, p. 83,) that which "is necessary to the existence of all other particular sensations, and that may exist independently of the nervous system ;"—we may accept the statement as practically applicable to the purpose of Christian culture. Some maxims based upon this distinction, may put the subject in a clearer light, *viz.*,

First. In all mental depressions, and impulsive wandering of thoughts a physical cause should be suspected when no moral cause can be detected.

Second. When the mental impressions are in opposition to conscience and the law of our affections, and when argument and will have no commanding effect, it is tolerably certain that the cause is physical.

Third. When prayer conjoined with will and effort, produce only a very transient exemption, or none at all, the physical origin of the difficulty is beyond a doubt. The remedy then is—to get *cured* if possible, or, in the absence of such possibility, to bear the depression, or the wandering thoughts as any other *affliction* would be borne— as a part of life's discipline, to be sanctified through our patience and trust, to our good. "You will never cure them" (wandering thoughts) "by set reflections; . . . be simply content to yield your will to God without reservation, and when any state of suffering is brought before you, accept it as his will, in an absolute abandonment to his guidance." Fenelon "*Christian Counsel.*"

(5) The experience of Christian Holiness is not an undisturbed calm.

Peace may "flow as a river," but even the river has its waves breaking backward as it meets the upward rush of the sea, or feels the pressure of the wind against its flow. So, the really calm heart may be surface-tossed while the great roll of its tide is toward God.

(6) Neither does this experience imply an absence of painful and unreasonable emotions. If the reader has noted carefully what was said about our inability to control our thoughts, he will be prepared to accept this statement, *viz.*, Our emotional natures are so under the dominion of our physical states and of circumstances, that they are often impressed, even contrary to our will and efforts.

How many sincere Christians have at times felt to an altogether unreasonable extent the heart-yearnings of home-sickness? One of the most devoted women whom we have met, narrated to us her own experience when her youngest daughter went to a distant place to school. Her *feelings* were those of one *bereaved* of her child. Her appetite failed; a terrible gloom settled upon her spirits; and notwithstanding her utmost efforts to be cheerful for the sake of her remaining daughters and for the honor of her religion, she was utterly absorbed in a sad sense of *loss* that nothing could mitigate. She is one of the most cheerful of women, and the clearness of her views and experience of Christian holiness is rarely equalled; yet for days she continued in this mood which was at last dispelled as suddenly as it appeared, but neither in its coming or stay, had it stained the purity of her spirit.

The writer is acquainted with a Christian lady sixty-one years of age, in sufficient health to care for her family unaided, who, all her life, has been subject to uncontrollable nervousness, especially during thunder showers. From the first rumbling of the thunder until it is all over, she is faint, pallid, and can do nothing but walk the floor or sit and wring her numb and bloodless hands. Yet she has no fear of the lightning, and no fear of death. It is to her an unaccountable peculiarity. Yet her mother who died at ninety-two was similarly affected. Our own theory is that the grandmother, gave the lunatic nerves to the mother through some terrible fright connected with thunder by the law of impressional heredity (see pp. 110-114), and thus the daughter and granddaughter have suffered.

This lady is a devoted Christian earnestly yearning and striving—habitually—for sanctifying grace. Yet, all through her religious life she has been occasionally doing things (seemingly whimsical, prejudiced or even resentful) that have subjected her to severe criticism for want of consistency. As she once phrased it in class meeting, she has "been the victim of circumstances." We have no desire to apologize for inconsistency, but we cannot forget that those thunder-shower nerves *are her work-day nerves;* more, that they are the machinery and the *only* machinery by which her really loving Christian spirit is geared to physical life. May it not be, therefore, that the "inconsistencies" complained of belong to the same class of *spinal reactions*, pp. 45-46, or nerve-lunacy, as that other inconsistency—namely—a Christian woman walking the floor and wringing her hands in a thunderstorm as if she had no Father above and no heaven to go to! Since the above was written, this lady has a very clear and definite experience of heart-cleansing, yet her nerves remain the same and unreasonable emotion still sometimes holds sway.

"Oh, Lord, take my heart, for I cannot give it, and when thou hast it, O keep it, for I cannot keep it for thee, and save me in spite of myself, for Jesus Christ's sake"—was the prayer of one who evidently failed to make the discrimination here insisted upon. If the reader will return to page 52 he will find the physiological reason for the preceding statements in what is there called the "organic element" of emotion.

(7.) From what has already been said it follows that—entire freedom from peevish tempers is not to be looked for. Mr. Youatt relates his experience with a horse in rabies thus—"He would bend his gaze upon me as if he would search me through and through and would prevail on me, if I could, to relieve him from some dreadful evil by which he was threatened. He would then press his head against my bosom and keep it there for a minute or more." "Yet in the paroxysms this touching desire for sympathy ... would change almost instantaneously into the most maddened fury, or else the most singular treachery.... Not a motion is made by the bystanders of which the rabid horse is not conscious, nor does a person approach him whom he does not recognize; but he labors under one all-absorbing feeling—an intense longing to devastate and destroy. His natural disposition is overborne by the power of the disease."

It is well known that in cases of tumor in adults, and disease of the hip-joint in children, distressing dreams are the mental result, while, in even the healthy, the irritability that follows a night of dissipation is matter of common remark. Chronic dyspepsia, or habitual exhaustion of the nervous energies by excessive labor, or the use of narcotics have the same effect.

But what bearing can these facts have upon our subject? This: If the disposition of a horse can be changed by disease, if tumors and inflamed joints can beget bad dreams, if dyspepsia and riotous excess can cause irritability, then the sanctified mother whose unremitting toils through the day, followed by a night or nights of wakefulness, watching, and anxiety, and all this perhaps amid the indescribable life-drain of a healthy infant tugging at the breast of a weakly mother, surely all this may induce a physical condition of which irritability is as truly *symptomatic* as headache is of a foul stomach.

There is an essential difference between a nervous function and muscular power. By frequent exercise the muscular system *increases* in strength and *decreases* in irritability; but the nerve force, by repeated calls upon it, *increases* in irritability, and *decreases* in strength.

Says Dr. Maudsley, "*Physiology and Pathology of Mind,*" p. 83 : " No culture of the mind, however careful, no effort of the will, however strong, will avail to prevent irregular and convulsive action when a certain degree of instability of nervous element has, from one cause or another, been produced in the spinal cells. It would be equally absurd to preach control to the spasms of chorea, or restraint to the convulsions of epilepsy, or to preach moderation to the east wind, or gentleness to the hurricane. That which in such case has its foundation in a definite physical cause must have its cure in the production of a definite physical change."

In genuine sanctification these temporary aberations of disposition or emotions are *marked by no endorsement of the will*, and usually by some discoverable abnormal condition of the body, or by some known derangement of the nerves.

(8.) A state of holiness does not denote the absence of sense-deceptions.

That very great acuteness is imparted to the senses sometimes in certain conditions has been observed by all physicians.

W. Derham, " *Physico-Theology,*" p. 304, gives

some instances, one of which was that of a gentleman whose eyes were diseased, and the sense of sight became so keen that he could distinguish colors in the dark. It would not be strange, therefore, if sense deceptions were sometimes the consequence of disease. As a matter of fact, surgeons well know that injuries to the brain frequently cause false reports of the senses. What Sir John Herschel calls " Visual images in darkness," (see " *Lectures on Scientific Subjects,*") is still more to our purpose, for they " are waking impressions, in perfect health, and under no sort of excitement,—geometrical forms, landscapes, human faces, etc., appearing to him in the darkness.

The writer is frequently subject to the same class of impressions. Sometimes no sooner are our eyes closed in perfect darkness than the most strange, grotesque, and amusing images will appear fully formed and most perfect in distinctness, and instantly vanish, to be followed by others so totally dissimilar as to have no other relation than that of mere succession. We often laugh outright at the comical display. At other times the images are grave, or beautiful, but always complete and instantly gone. In our own case they almost always occur after a period of intense thought. But they have nothing whatever to do with holiness of heart.

(9.) The complete extinguishment of morbid appetites is not necessarily implied in heart-purity. There is a disease called Bulimia, in which "the patient is affected with an inordinate appetite, which nothing can satiate, and which his will seems powerless to resist." "*Philosophical Transactions*," vol. 22, gives an account of a man who would eat an ordinary leg of veal besides thistles and other wild vegetables, at a single meal.

Another would eat raw rats, cats, and dogs, and candles to the extent of fourteen pounds daily. (*London Med. and Physical Journal.*)

We have known two cases, one of which would disgust the reader to recite, and the other is strikingly illustrative of our proposition, because he was a man of genuine piety, and otherwise spotless character. Yet he would steal in the night to his employer's larder—after eating as much during the day as two or three ordinary men—and devour several links of raw sausage at a time. A sanctified soul may have a body sufficiently under the power of disease to exhibit some morbid appetite. Dr. Van de Warker, "*Popular Science Monthly*, No. 39, says: "In those cases—and they are *not* rare—in which the organic appetites affect unduly and too persistently the consciousness, it becomes the source of great unhappiness, or of bad health." Early wrong habits, or a baneful heritage of evil, has stamped upon the whole nervous organism an abnormal sensibility to organic processes that becomes a blight of hopelessness as to the attainment of the serene state of rest supposed to pertain to a life of holiness. Let no victim of this unfortunate condition confound an experience of purity with exemption from disease or its consequences.

(10.) It is not implied in heart-purity that there shall be complete control of nervous agitations.

"Nervous health is one thing, and moral health is another. We suspect that what is good for the one is often bad for the other." "*London Spectator.*"

Every organ in the body is endowed with the property of irritability, *i. e.*, re-acting in some peculiar manner to the action of a direct stimulus. Thus the glands show their re-action by increased secretions; the capillary vessels by congestion; the muscles by contraction, and the nerves by sensations or movements.

Enough has already been said to show that in an unhealthy condition of nerves, corresponding pains or agitations are the natural result, and this result is no index to the state of the heart.

(11.) Sanctification does not suppose an entire absence of spasmodic muscular movements.

Dr. Laycock has shown that "involuntary muscular movements take place in respondence not merely to sensations, but to ideas; and not merely at the prompting of ideas actually before the mind, but through the action of the substrata left by past mental operations. Thus, for example the convulsive paroxysm of hydrophobia may be excited not merely by the sight and sound of water, but by the *idea* of water suggested either by a picture or by the verbal mention of it." *London Quarterly Review,* Oct. 1871. See also pp 45, and 46 of this work.

There is a singular disease—St. Vitus Dance— insanity of the muscles—indicating an unhealthy state of the co-ordinating power, (see page 48,) which may co-exist with the purest moral character. The reflex power of nerve-centers has been explained upon page 41 and all that now needs to be added is to remind the reader that sanctification is a moral state within the realm of physical laws.

What then *is* involved in the experience of Christian Holiness?

Answer: We are not to attempt the impracticable. E. g., If certain nervous disorders or hereditary conditions afflict us, we are to accept the facts as they are and suit our efforts to the possibilities of the case, (see pp 126-128), and not endeavor to fit one garment of purity to all distorted forms. We should ascertain surely what is vulnerable and what is invulnerable and not waste our power in vain.

How shall we discriminate? "When organic processes which ordinarily go on without consciousness force themselves into consciousness (by a sense of weariness, heaviness, pain, etc.,) it is the certain mark of a vital degeneration." *Maudsley*. In all such cases an unsatisfactory experience should be sifted thoroughly for *mental effects of disease*. Then the maxims laid down on pp. 213–214, by which to distinguish voluntary from involuntary thoughts should be applied, and it may be confidently assumed that an intelligent course of investigation like this will soon settle the question.

2. Rightly distribute the work to be done. That work is—Believing and doing. Believing for anything needed provided there is a clear promise or a valid inference justifying the faith, and *working* in all practicable spheres when faith cannot preserve us with a spotless conscience, and glorify God as he requires.

But care must be exercised to keep each in its place. Faith must not arrogate to herself all the virtue of christian character, and Works—because more tangible—must not assume to be the entire substance of Christian life.

So, Believing and Working belong to man; Saving and Co-working pertain to God. The spheres may intermingle in a thousand directions but every separate thread of responsibility holds its continuity with its Divine or human source, and while to the observer all may seem an inextricable tangle of inexplicable questions, to the all-piercing eye of Moral obligation the distribution is as accurate as fact, and as important as destiny, and with the Divine Promise especially applicable just here, "He shall lead you into all truth," no humble child of His need ever to despair of being able rightly to distribute the work to be done.

3. Do your part faithfully. With *fidelity*, because a lack of fidelity is to that extent treachery to the high interests committed to your trust. No Christian seeking purity of life as a fitting complement of purity of spirit, can harbor treachery without an instantaneous surrender of his professed object.

Do that part *now*, because this moment only is your own: and even it flies as you gaze upon it —not to be lost only, but to *stamp the coming moment with its own character.*

The future can be provided for only by taking

care of the present. Every fleeting instant leaves a mold into which the plastic succeeding instant runs and takes its form. Let Fidelity cast these molds of the coming seconds, and they are stamped for God as they come, and they weave around the Christian heart a golden coat-of-mail every separate link of which has been forged in holy fires and tempered with heavenly skill. Duties made habit, is a complete reversal of the pre-inclinations of the heart. Especially is this true of fidelity to privilege in the baptism of the Holy Spirit. No Christian can afford to live without the wonder-working hand of the Holy Ghost upon him frequently, giving to these transfiguration hours a surpassing sweetness and a matchless power to permeate, exalt and spiritualize many after-days.

4. Trust God to do his part instantly. The point so strongly insisted upon in elaborating the elements of sanctifying faith (page 187) must be adverted to just here, and its importance emphasized as applying to the *whole course* of sanctified life. God's co-working will be found to be just as much dependent upon your assumption of his trustworthiness in your Christian activities, as his sanctifying grace was in the glorious hour of your heart-cleansing. Hence, an expectation of his in-

stantaneous co-operation should be the *habitual* state of mind in which duty should be performed.

3. *Admonitory of the dangers.*

1. A very general one is: Dallying with temptation. Not that it is peculiar to a life of entire devotedness; on the contrary, *when recognized*, it is excluded from such a life, but the danger is that the temptation will appear in some form so disguised that it will seem to be a legitimately debatable question, and thus hold the mind to its consideration until it has awakened a desire in the same direction. The true policy is to bring all such things immediately to the test of the Word and the Spirit's guidance, pleading the promise, "If any among you lack wisdom," etc., and giving the benefit of the doubt, if there be such, to self-denial and purity rather than to indulgence. Dr. McCabe, "*Light on the Pathway of Holiness*," p. 80, shows that the temptations of the sanctified are usually to "an excessive action or indulgence of sensibilities in themselves innocent and proper." And page 46 of this treatise points to a large and powerful class of temptations that may arise from physical causes. Rev. J. D. Tettey in "*Scriptural Holiness*, (London,) has an admirable chapter clearly stating the distinction often made between a tempting object as recognized by the perceptions,

as felt by the sensibilities, and as consented to by the will, and correctly insists that *prior to the consent of the will*, there is no sin. Yet the consent of the will may be to simple dalliance but not indulgence—a position of great danger to, if not positive destruction of, heart-purity.

2. Another danger is that of Resting in partial success. A glorious victory has been achieved, and substantial conquest gained, but consolidation in the new condition of things must be experienced. The old habits have been eradicated, but the new need to be confirmed. Hence progress is imperative. No pause for self-gratulation can be allowed. The new recruits of thoughts and feelings must be thoroughly drilled to hold as well as occupy their new possession, but hold it only as vantage ground for movements still further in advance. The campaign is organized upon the plan of no retrogression. "Conquer, hold, forward," is the standing order of the chief. No partial success, however glorious, can be obedience. On, *on* to the full consummation! That, and that alone is Sanctified Life. The assumption of final victory without unremitting effort is a delusion and a snare.

3. Another danger is the disposition to suppress distinct and positive testimony. "With the heart

man believeth unto righteousness, and with the mouth confession is made unto salvation," is a principle that applies to the whole course of Christian discipleship. Nor can any personal views of demerit, or real humility of spirit avail to excuse even the lowliest from the duty of rendering unto God the first fruits of praise in the presence of his people after each harvesting of grace. Not that the statements should be made indiscriminately; on the contrary, always with a wise reference to circumstances as indices of God's will. But at proper times the testimony should be clear, explicit, and with humble reliance upon Him to "establish" the "word in the mouth of two or three witnesses."

As to the *value* of such testimony, Rev. Dr. Major, "*Christian Perfection*," pp. 87-92, has summarized in a most conclusive form all that need to be said upon that point.

4. The habitual repression of the emotions is another danger, of special magnitude in these days of prim propriety and conventional usurpation in Christian devotion.

"When the sensorium is strongly excited, nerve-force is generated in great excess." *Darwin.*

That the sensorium (pp. 47-48) should be thus excited is but a natural result of the condition of the earnest Christian amid the play of the mightiest forces that ever visit the heart of man. The stupendous claims of God, the comprehensive devotement of self, the melting appeals of Infinite Love, the majestic mandates of all obligation, the supreme importance of eternal interests, the audacious insolence of satanic interference, the outrageous perversions of carnal self-life—all these crowding the arena of thought and impulse and emotion, in one brief hour of service—surely if the sensorium have any sensibility its most lethargic cells will thrill with activity now, and that activity "will generate nerve-force in great excess," *i. e.*, in excess of the ordinary measure. The nerve-force thus generated *must go somewhere and do something.*

It may expend itself in mere emotion, or it may arouse the emotions only that they may be the stimulus to corresponding actions, or it may stir the emotions, and then be reflected in the action of the hemispheres as repressive volition forcing the emotions into hasty submission. "Emotion, unless directed in proper channels is highly destructive to the stability of the nervous centers." When, therefore, the nerve-force awakens emotions which expend themselves in their own exercise, it is a "highly destructive" process. When the nerve force arouses first the emotions and then the will to quell the ebulitions it is no less a "highly destructive" process, because the emotions are not "directed," but repressed.

Therefore, the physiological, the psychological, the Christian use of such emotions is to *direct them in channels which their own instincts select.* If those emotions be kindled in private devotion and take the form of thanks-giving, let the voice of thanks-giving—Praise—be the natural, and none the less saintly, product. If they be aroused in public worship, and the sympathies melt at the condition of the unsaved, let those sympathies find their appropriate expression in sympathetic words of warning or invitation, or deeds of winning influence and power. But beware of the suggestion that this work should be transferred to other hands.

It is *your* nerve-force that is generated in excess, and *that cannot* be transferred to another! Neither can it be wrongly used without a direct *spiritual* as well as physical injury.

This treatise will have been in vain as far as you are concerned, if you have not already been convinced that the realms of the physical and the spiritual interpenetrate each other to such an extent that no great law of either can be violated without the other receiving an injury of corresponding magnitude. But if any should fail to comprehend the importance of this view, we call to their attention the fact that *emotions habitually repressed at last lose their power.* Here is a mental law that cannot be ignored. Spiritual emotions have their place, and a most important one it is, in the economy of individual salvation. To repress them, therefore, habitually, is to revolutionize God's plan of saving us, and to substitute a device of our own. But God will not yield the sceptre; hence Barrenness and Powerlessness sit as twin daughters of Folly watching the warring zeal of multitudes who "did run well for a season," but who made the wretched mistake of supposing that they could "do God service" by stamping upon the flaming brands which his own truth and spirit kindled, in obedience to the behests of timid worldly conservatism.

5. Beware of seeking a quiescent peace. Possibly there may be a few—a very few peculiarly constituted ones, who are called to a contemplative, intro-spective, self-gratulatory quiescence, while the great world storms around, and the mass of believers feel constrained to seize the ropes, and work the pumps and man the guns in something more than a waking dream-life of pleasant trust.

This is a work-day world, and he who gives his heart to God in utter self-abandonment consents thereby to be thrown bodily right into the thick of whatever activity can be most and best affected by his presence and exertions. Let the sick rest. Let the stupid dream. Let the visionary mount their chariots of moonbeams and soar whither they will, but as for us, let us remember that the day is for work.

6. In steering clear of the quicksand of quiescence, be careful to avoid the rock of fanaticism.

Holiness is supremely a *one idea* theme. And one ideaists are in peculiar danger of extremes. Hence it is that the good cause is so fearfully weighted with so many really good but run-to-seed Christians, and so many constitutional hobbyists to whom a one idea truth of real magnitude is a Mecca of life-long aspiration. Its sober and balanced advocates must needs suffer somewhat from this unavoidable condition of things, but should be all the more on their guard not to add to the difficulties by their own indiscretions. It were well for all to read carefully Mr. Wesley's caution against " enthusiasm " in his " *Plain Account of Christian Perfection,*" pp. 135-139.

7. Canting pietism should be carefully avoided. Conviction may be spoken, testimony may be given, exhortations may be uttered, and prayers may be offered brim full of the very marrow of clear, distinct, and conscious salvation without

once trenching upon the shriveled and repulsive domain of Cant. Set phrases, in affected style and whining tones is bad enough anywhere, but in advocacy of the greatest boon of God to men it is ridiculous, and but for the good intentions involved would be detestable. "Let your yea be yea, and your nay be nay," and leave the mouthings of stereotyped affectation to those who have no better capital.

Say Dr. D. Curry, "*Perfect Love,*" p. 42: "A special dialect should be avoided as far as possible.... It is the easiest thing in the world to fall into the use of words without definite meaning. This evil is greatly intensified when it is accompanied by a mannerism of tones, and methods of utterance, and unmeaning and unnecessary peculiarities."

CHAPTER II.

THE SUBJECT PRACTICALLY APPLIED.

1. *To the private Christian.*

1. As an experience personally needed.

Whether we consider the almost universal lack of power to master the evil tendencies within, and to pass unharmed through those without; or the co-extensive service-life of hard duties and unwelcome crosses, smothering the feeble joy that struggles for existence, and putting far off the exultant victory that should crown Christian sonship with perpetual triumph; the need is too apparent for argument.

We appeal, therefore, to the consciousness of the reader, and calling to remembrance the glorious aspirations of the past—holding him face to face with the spirit-kindled yearnings within, and pointing to the promises all-glorious with the purity which they pledge, for assurance; to the experiences all-lustrous in the moral beauty which they illustrate, for encouragement; to the baptisms of power, surcharged with overmastering might of God, for reliance;* to the outmost reaching, deep-most cleansing blood of Jesus, for the all-perfect washing—we cry, " My God shall supply all your NEED, according to his riches in glory by Christ Jesus." Wondrous supply—the supply of God. Wondrous measure—triplicate as his own nature!

---

*Baptisms of the Holy Ghost are defined by Rev. Henry Belden thus: " Refreshings, quickenings, spiritual holy impulses given at any stage of the Christian life." Rev. B. W. Gorham—"*God's Method with Men,*" p. 235—adds: "With each successive coming of the Spirit there is always an experience which places the soul in a new position beyond what it had reached before."

"According to his GLORY." As wide as his own omnipresence! As enduring as his own eternity!! Earth-time is but a speck upon the infinite expanse. Yet, we in time—filling not the billionth part of that speck even—what can we comprehend of that illimitable glory?

But that is only the initial step in the measurement. "According to his glory by CHRIST JESUS." All the boundless sea of his immeasurable and interminable glory made phosphorescent in the glow of the character and work of Jesus Christ, as the long-sufferingness of Love stands unveiled before all intelligences, and things "which the angels desired to look into" are revealed.

Beyond all this—"according to the RICHES of his glory by Christ Jesus." Wealth of worth incalculable! Wealth of praise how sumless! Wealth of delight how ineffable!

In view of such a measure, well may God declare: "For as the heavens are higher than the earth, so are my ways higher than your ways, and my thoughts than your thoughts." How much this means let him illustrate in hearts emptied and trusting in his hands, in the attitude expressed by Frances Ridley Havergal in her personal covenant of July 1876:

"Now Lord I give myself to thee,

I would be wholly thine;
As thou hast given thyself to me,
And thou art wholly mine;
O take me, seal me as thine own,
Thine altogether—thine alone."

2. As an experience certainly attainable.

It were useless to quote scripture passages in confirmation of this assertion, for they must necessarily be INTERPRETED, and it is well known that some schools of theology find it easy to give to any that might be cited, a signification entirely different from our own. But there is a kind of evidence that cannot be explained away without utterly destroying the credibility of all testimony. The oral and printed statements of the number who profess to know this as a fact of experience, constitutes a mass of evidence which no sane man who carefully considers, can innocently gainsay. The witnesses are from all ranks of society, of all grades of culture, of all degrees of refinement, of all adult years, of all shades of temperament, of all varieties of previous Christian character. And their statements are concerning facts of consciousnes, lying within its legitimate domains which are corroberated by marked contemporary changes of deportment, and subsequent adherence to their views, and consistency of life with them, which together furnishes proof as conclusive as anything human can be. If, however, the analytic mind needs or desires further confirmation, it is found in the philosophy of the subject as presented in this volume, for no error can be wrought into a consistent and harmonious philosophical system.

Now let us trace an experience through its several phases.

Suppose a penitent at God's altar to be moulded as He pleases. The consecration has been complete, and now the soul is passive in the hands of a God who hates sin with all the loathing of his infinite nature, and loves holiness with a corresponding intensity. The will of the penitent is not merely acquiescent but concurrent in any process that may be needful for his salvation. He is believing. He is saved.

A few days pass away and he feels nothing wrong within. But suddenly, in a moment of temptation, anger arises, or covetousness grasps, or profanity struggles for expression. He is astounded, overwhelmed, almost in despair.

He is told that he now " needs the second blessing." What is implied in this, he has little conception of; but he seeks earnestly for deliverance, and is greatly blessed. He feels these besetments no more, and is told that he is cleansed from sin. A few months pass away, and although anger, covetousness and profanity are all destroyed, pride begins to inflate, and again he is bewildered. He is told that he has lost his hold; that he must seek the second blessing over again. He tries again, and receives another baptism of the Spirit, and pride is expelled. Time passes, and although he cannot doubt the victories that he has achieved, now ambition begins to urge, and again the poor man is in trouble. Twice already he has thought himself cleansed from all the " roots of bitterness ;" and lo! ambition dwells within! Still, he thinks that somehow—he scarcely knows how—he must have been unfaithful, and again he seeks the cleansing blood, and is saved.

Those workings of the "carnal nature" that he first felt after his conversion were the preponderating habits of his soul, which filled all the foreground of his consciousness, so that his attention was completely absorbed by them, and his first cleansing was simply the sanctification of those habits. But when they were revolutionized, pride, which had been lurking back unobserved because of the prominence of the others, appeared in view; and the second cleansing was the sanctification of that habit. And then ambition deployed its forces, and that was sanctified. And so the process might continue as long as any unsanctified habit remained. And the work might proceed in any order that the necessities of the case might demand.

But why does not God sanctify our habits in regeneration? Because it would be a violation of the laws of our mental nature, amidst the surroundings of *this life*, to entirely sanctify the *my* in regeneration.

In penitence the will is *usually* not sufficiently engaged with habits to secure their eradication. Sometimes, indeed, the soul may be partially sanctified in its habits in regeneration, in those cases where the sinful habit has been a special burden, and is an object of loathing, but even then no further than the *will voluntarily and definitely allies itself with grace for this particular purpose*. Precisely the same truth applies to those cases of partial sanctification which occur subsequent to conversion. *Grace sanctifies just so far as, and no farther than, the will definitely concurs.* On page 49 it is shown that the hemispheres of the brain are "the material instruments through which the immaterial spirit operates," and on page 50, that the will "seems to stand to the hemispheres in the place of a higher nervous center." Therefore, a physical and psychological - *channel* is made for sanctifying grace in the alliance of the will of the subject with the

ITS PHILOSOPHY AND EXPERIENCE. 241

Holy Spirit. Perhaps the fact stated on page 51, that "the idea that a structural defect will certainly be removed by a particular act does sometimes so affect the organic action of the part as to produce a cure," may be taken as an illustration.

Suppose here is an individual with an inveterate blood disease that has been forming a painful tumor, and has also induced a craving for some noxious drug, which has been indulged in till the habit is fully formed, and its use reacts and aggravates the disease. Let the disease stand for the sinfulness of the nature, the tumor for out-breaking sin, the craving for the appetite, and the indulgence for the habit. Now, suppose a physician proposes to cure the patient by dissecting out the tumor (repentance), and purification of the blood by alteratives (regeneration), as a natural result the craving which sprang from the disease will cease. All this is done; yet shortly after the operation the patient complains that the physician has not done his work thoroughly, because he feels his old desire for the drug, which he thinks is incompatible with a pure state of the blood. The physician replies: The tumor is removed; your blood is perfectly pure, and what you feel is only the old habit of indulgence. The craving does not now arise from the state of your blood, but from the fact that you have been addicted to the use of the drug. That is a law of mind which must be met by *will power*. Physic cannot remove it, but you can *will* it out! If you will undertake it, I may assist you by some gentle stimulants that will tend to form new appetites; but there must be absolute cessation of indulgence, and stern and persistent effort on your part.

Now the question might arise: Is the patient under any obligation to attempt his part of the assigned task?

If, by the habit of indulgence, he injures health and usefulness, and thus fails in his duty to others, he is most certainly responsible for that failure.

So, if by the continuance of old sinful habits we entail upon ourselves spiritual infirmity, and by that weakness fail in our duty to others; and if, above all else, our voluntarily perpetuated habits defile the outgoings of the pure spirit which God has placed within us, and we thus dishonor his workmanship, condemnation must be our inevitable doom. The dilemma is not, Advance, or fail to reach a glorious privilege! but, Advance, or lose our justification.

The work of sanctification now stands before us, not in the form of an intangible something to be acquired somehow, but as a plainly defined struggle and a consciously ascertained victory.

Is the body subjected to any unhealthy and depraving appetite? If so, it is vain for him to talk of being a "free man in Christ Jesus" until he emancipates himself from that humiliating thraldom. Oh, that all readers might be induced just here and now to bury the instruments of slavery of those old habits forever! Oh, that the *man*, the blood-redeemed *man*, would rise in rebellion against the dominancy of appetite! Your tobacco, your wine, your lust, your gluttony—lawful though they may be—righteous, *sanctified they never can be as* HABITS OF INDULGENCE, and innocent they cannot be while defiling and shattering the temple of the Holy Ghost!

Is your mind the slave of anger, petulance, censoriousness, envy, pride, ambition, covetousness? Here is your work. A mighty, desperate work it is! You cannot take that sinful habit and lay it at your bidding. You may bid it *down*, but it will up and taunt you with your weakness! You know that this is so. We do but tear a leaf from your own experience and read it to you now.

"What, then, shall I do?" Is this your cry? Wait a little.

Perhaps these depravities are hereditary, inborn, but strengthened by indulgence. So much the deeper is their hold! So much the firmer are you bound!

But habits can be eradicated in two ways: (1) By voluntary, gradual obliteration and substitution. You cannot will them away, but you can will them down, *and substitute them out! By substitution only comes deliverance.*

If the habit be physical, the substitutionary process need not be another indulgence less objectionable, but simply the healthful action of the organs implicated. If it be mental or spiritual, the energy that has flowed in that direction must find other and sanctified outlets.

This process of substitution is usually subject to two laws:

a. That of Impression, which has special relation to the habit first selected as the subject of experiment. *E. g.*, If anger is the predominating propensity, the impression of that fact is more clearly defined within the consciousness than any other, and therefore, when the work of transformation commences, it will seem to be mostly centered there. And, when acomplished there, the work may seem to be complete until the same law reveals some other depravity; and so on until the last old sinful habit is extirpated;

then, and not till then, is the soul sanctified entirely!

b. The law of Inspiration. All processes of human nature—physical, mental and spiritual—are quickened by inspiration. An aspiring thought will flash in the eye, tremble in the pulse, dance in the muscular movements, and chase away fatigue. Inspiration heightens the glow of Poesy, gives firmness to the tread of Reason, kindles the yearnings of Devotion, and stays the wanderings of Will. So the mighty work of sanctifying substitution quickens under the divinely kindled impulses of Inspiration. Hence, those means of grace that breathe the purest, strongest inspiration should be most relied upon in this warfare against depravity.

But all this speaks of time, and toil, and conflict. Aye, and of *peril* also; for old habits have a reactionary power over spirit-purity, so that it is quite possible that you may contract guilt by unnecessary delay, and thus your substitutionary process be more than neutralized by acquired pollution. Is there not a better way? Must we spend a lifetime in the sanctifying process, and be able to bring forth its glorious fruitage only in the sunset of our day? Or, worse still, should our day end at its meridian, can we never, *never* show to the world what it is perishing to see—the sanctifying graces of the Holy Spirit adorning all our earthly life? Yes! Glory to the Lamb! *There is a shorter way!* Not, perhaps to gain all victories at once, but, at least, to find all peace within the range of present consciousness and obligation.

(2) Habits may be removed by *revolutionary and supernatural substitution!*

By this we mean that the Divine Spirit can, *in a single moment*, with the concurrence of your will and the appropriations of your faith, work a change in your habits that shall be equivalent to your own disciplined substitution. The Holy Spirit can dig new channels for your activities in an instant, so that you who are so passionate, and who, under ordinary operations of grace, would require months or years of conflict in which to completely change your temper, may have that temper sanctified, in the twinkling of an eye, by the revolutionary processes of the Holy Ghost.

Rev. Dr. Asa Graham cites a case which illustrates this truth. He was a man of much means, but who had been, up to the time of his conversion, an intense miser. Greedy covetousness had been the all-controlling indwelling sin of his life. After his conversion he felt bound to contribute liberally for the cause of Christ. Every gift conferred, however, wrung his heart with agony.

Parting with his money was like parting with his life-blood. One class of teachers would have told this man that the good fight of faith with him would consist in resisting and holding in subjection such feelings, and in despite of the evil promptings, to give as God requires. Being taught by others "the way of the Lord more perfectly," "he went and told Jesus" of his evil case, and asked him to take away wholly, not only this indwelling sin, but to "save him unto the uttermost." The result was "a renewing of the Holy Ghost." From that hour, "giving to the poor," and "dispersing abroad," became the luxury of his life. The joy of his heart was to give as the Lord had prospered him.

Dr. Graham continues: The "easily besetting sin" of the celebrated theologian of America, Dr. Hopkins, was a very violent and easily excited temper. This propensity held despotic power over him, until after he had been for years in the ministry. On one occasion, he did great injury to his own peace and the cause of truth, under the influence of excited anger. The entire subsequent night he spent in prayer and humiliation, beseeching God to utterly annihilate in him that evil temper. Quite thirty years after that memorable night, that man of God testified, that during all this period he had never in a single instance, been conscious of the least stirring of an angry feeling or sentiment in his mind.

Is this doubted? Upon what ground? Is the faith that has looked out of darkness, and alienation, and guilt, and claimed Christ as a Savior, now incompetent to look from adoption, and childhood, and affinity, and claim Jesus as a sanctifier? Is the spirit, whose mighty energies have quickened the spirit into life, insufficient now to purify its belongings? Must the thousands upon thousands of God's saints, who in the past have thought themselves examples of this wondrous transformation, be classed with enthusiasts and self-deceivers? No, no! When we reflect upon these things, and consider the positive affirmations of those who testified so explicitly upon this point, and then, more satisfactorily than all else, bring to mind our own experience of the revolutionary power of the Holy Spirit, we feel that "To doubt would be disloyalty; to falter would be sin." And, therefore, we proclaim to you again, with redoubled emphasis, the glorious truth that what will cannot do alone, and will and substitution can only do after long and painful struggles, the new-creating, soul-baptizing, habit-changing Spirit can do, with the concurrence of your will and faith, *just here and now*. Hear it, ye tempted ones! Hear it, ye struggling ones!

Hear it, ye defeated ones! The all-conquering Spirit waits!

But you must first consecrate yourself as fully, as formally, as irrevocably, as much in detail, as if you were making inventory to deed yourself away for gold. And the spirit, life and power of your consecration must consist in this: that your will freely and forever accepts God's will as its one, sole, changeless *law!* Do you do it? Now, the crowning of your consecration must be in here and now committing your faith-faculty, your power of believing, your present trust, to the Word of God, in present acceptance of his sanctifying grace. Is this done? Then do not look in upon yourself to see what the effect is. That is going by sight, not by faith! Hold on by faith; and though you have no evidence of feeling still believe, and keep believing; and while believing, though Satan comes he shall find nothing in you. God's word is evidence enough for faith

Some of you are sanctified in part. Some habits have been slain. Some are still alive. By the numbers of the dead you may compute the *my* already sanctified. By the presence of the living you may estimate the magnitude of the work before you. Ah, how sadly your Achans have discomfited Israel! We charge you, men of God, bring every one to the stoning-place! Dare not, upon your peril, dare not to carry one along with you. It will be a blighting, withering curse to you! Come, then, with your "wedge of gold and Babylonish garment!" Heaven help you now! Jesus stands by! The Mighty Helper aids! The sanctifying Spirit breathes upon us! Now, now, we die to sin! We crucify self! We bury old habits! We live to God! The blood cleanses? Our hearts rest! We are saved—*saved*—SAVED in Him!

> "'T is done; Thou do'st this moment save—
>   With full salvation bless;
> Redemption through Thy blood I have,
>   And spotless love, and peace."

3. As peculiarly affecting the marriage relation.

We omit all insistance upon the *spirit* which it imparts to domestic life as too obvious to need comment, and pass at once to the consideration of a branch of the subject rarely, if ever before, made prominent in the treatment of this great theme. We refer to the duty of sanctified parents to beget children *better* by nature than themselves.

Says I. Taylor, "*Nat. Hist. of Enthusiasm*," p. 142:

"On principles even of mathematical calculation, each individual of the human family may be demonstrated to hold in his hand the center lines of an interminable web-work, on which are sustained the fortunes of multitudes of his successors. These implicated consequences, if summed together, make up therefore a weight of human weal or woe that is reflected back with an incalculable momentum upon the lot of each."

That some marriages doom children before they are born is grimly implied in the oft-quoted language of Dr. Holmes—"There are people who think that every thing may be done, if the doer, be he educator or physician, be only called in season. No doubt—but *in season* would often be a hundred or two years before the child was born."

Impressed with the importance of this view, Fernald says in "*First Causes of Character*," p. 57: "If clergymen would .... only occasionally, which they might with the utmost propriety, unfold the laws of nature, which are the laws of God, in the spiritual and physical connections of human pairs, they might dispense with a large part of their theology; for nature itself would become so practical, exact, and regular, that the God of nature would work through it without obstruction, and the Holy Spirit find an almost involuntary entrance."

We quote this language, not endorsing it in all its strength, but as indicating a vast field of truth too much neglected.

Henry C. Wright may not be regarded as high authority by the advocates of Christian Holiness generally, but a truth is a truth by whomsoever uttered, and such is his statement, namely:

"What is *organized* into us, in our pre-natal state, is of more consequence to us, and more vital to our triumph over the temptations and obstacles that impede our progress toward perfection and happiness, than what is *educated* into us after we are born."

It is concerning the badly organized unfortunates that Leckey says, "There are men whose lives are spent in willing one thing and desiring the opposite."

Dr. Bushnell wheels a whole battalion of trenchant words into the same line when he declares: "In our birth, we not only begin to breathe and circulate blood, but it is a question hugely significant, whose the blood may be. For in this we have whole rivers of predispositions, good or bad, set running in us—as much more powerful to shape our future than all tuitional and regulative influences that come after, as they are earlier in their beginning, deeper in their insertion, and more constant in their operation."

This truth, which cannot be successfully controverted, leads to a most important inference, namely: That the *largest possibilities of the improvement of the race gather into the moment of conception and the period before birth.* (See on "Heredity," pp. 109–114.) Just there focalize the elevating influences of education and regeneration, and a good first birth may be secured to the child by the discipline and second birth of the parent.

"It is the greatest part of our felicity to be well born." (Fernelius.)

After the first birth, "the aim of Christian education has been to piously bring up children in sin instead of allowing them to vegetate in it," whereas it should be to begin with the gift of a good first birth, trusting God to coincidently impart the second birth, and then from this lofty vantage ground, train them in a piety corresponding with their capacities. Thus eventually a long line of godly ancestry might result, from which a religious temperament might naturally and constitutionally proceed.

From this general survey let us return to individual responsibility. Every parent is projecting more or less of himself *within* the coming generation, therefore the part thus transmitted should be his best and noblest. Hence he should hold no sentiment, indulge no passion, form no habit, that he would not have organized as a predisposition into the nature of his child. Not content with this negative virtue, he should remember the wholesome words of Dr. Napheys on p. 218 of his "*Transmission of Life:*"

"We cannot by any course of virtue beget a child free from evil tendencies, but we can give him much to combat them through the virtuous qualities of civilization. The animal nature of man cannot be modified. It is invariably transmitted. It is always the same in the barbarian and in the enlightened man. But moral and mental qualities can be added, which, although they can never crush out nor wholly obscure the animal nature, *can improve upon it.*" And the extent of that possible improvement has already been sufficiently indicated.

2. *The subject applied to organized churches.*

1. As a formula of faith.

How much more beautiful and consistent with the *design of the church* is a creed which recognizes the truth of this doctrine, than one that denies it; and how much more it glorifies the grace of God, and inspires men with hope, may be seen by two contrasted formulated statements.

(1) CREED OF LIMITED SALVATION.

I believe that after regeneration there still remain "roots of bitterness"—remnants of the "carnal nature," which do and will all through life break out in actual sins, so that Christians are in continual need of the justifying grace of God, and cannot expect to be entirely saved from sin until the hour of death.

(2) CREED OF HOLINESS.

I believe that after regeneration there still remain "roots of bitterness"—remnants of the "carnal nature"—which are so liable to break out under the stimulus of satanic influences, (see pp. 73-74,) into actual sin, that Christians are invited to obtain the sanctifying grace of God, and be thenceforth preserved "blameless unto the coming of our Lord Jesus Christ."

Now, as a test of the relative correspondence of these creeds with the spontaneous instincts and the cultured aspirations of Christian hearts, let them be read in turn to one just exulting in the new-born joy of his conversion, and likewise to a mature disciple, faithful and zealous, and thirsting with unutterable desire to be conformed to the mind of Christ; and it needs no ken of prophecy to foresee which will best accord with the divinely-wrought states and impulses of each.

Then, let them be read again to a compromising professor, whose better feelings have long been buried beneath a mass of selfishness, and whose greatest anxiety is, first, to grasp the world, and then, to justify his conduct, and his choice may be as readily foreseen as can that of the other.

But can that be a truly Christian creed which so harmonizes with such an unchristian or, at best, poorly Christian life? And can that be a non-christian creed which so adequately meets and truly expresses the noblest and purest longings, and clearest perceptions of spirit-trained hearts?

If, then, the church has a faith, she should make haste to formulate it and thus avail herself of all the educative power that may result from its use.

2. As the mightiest force of evangelism.

The only power that the gospel has over the minds of men, is its power to save. Eliminate that, and all that remains is but ingenious fable, or, at best, historical romance. The hold which it has upon the conscience is its recognized ability to meet a pressing need, and the deeper that sense of need in any case, the stronger its grasp upon the spirit.

Experience proves that there is no deeper sense of need, none, indeed, marked by such unutterable yearnings, as those which characterize the strivings of the faithful Christian after purity.

The cry of penitence, it is true, sometimes sobs forth an anguish that seems hard by the borders of despair, and pleas for mercy that might melt a heart of stone, indicate how desperate is the want within; but the wild, instinctive shriek of the poor man who toppled over the rapids of Niagara, was as nothing to the mute appeals that his blanched face made, while, for hours he clung with the strength of desperation to the rock which he caught just above the terrific falls. So, the spirit's call for help when it first awakens to a realization of its sinfulness and peril, may be filled with the wild vehemence of terror, but it knows little of that deep, settled, self-loathing, that hungry, starving heart-ache, that consuming thirst of desire which wrestles through weary days, and waits through laggard nights, till, almost sick of hope deferred, and tired of life, in mute wretchedness of love, it wonders if there be any help this side of heaven! Ah, it is blessed to be able to point the weeping penitent to the Forgiving One; and it is glorious to be able to shout in the ear of the polluted, "I will sprinkle clean water upon you, and from *all your filthiness*, and from all your idols I will *cleanse you!*" *This* is a salvation that measures out to man's broadest need, and finds its crowning glory in its uttermost provisions! No wonder, then, that its loftiest challenge ofttimes arrests where its simple proffers pass unnoticed!

Sanctified men are God's veterans in his war against sin.

Militiamen may sometimes be relied upon to defend strongly fortified places, but when campaigns are to be fought through "on this line," men are needed who can face the glittering steel, "close up" in solid column when windrows fall, and when the bugle rings the charge, sweep like the march of Death, upon the foe.

So, when Life's test-hours come, when the decisive struggle verges to its culmination, God calls for hearts that are panoplied in steel, and that will stand amid the shocks of battle, and rush to the charge of Christian effort, like Napoleon's grand Old Guards who never knew defeat till they found it in annihilation.

As we were once crossing the City Hall Park, the sound of martial music fell upon our ears, and turning towards Broadway we saw some of the returning regiments of the Army of the Potomac, and as the bronzed and battle-scarred veterans filed into the Park, we stood and gazed upon them with overflowing eyes, as we thought of what they had dared and done for us.

At last, as the center of the column turned in, two flag-staffs, borne side by side, attracted our attention. Hanging from those staffs were the remnants of the battle-banners that had swept in alternate victory and defeat over the blood-soaked fields of the Peninsula, through the campaigns of Maryland and the Rappahannock, amid the terrible death-grapples of the Wilderness, and over the ramparts of Petersburg, and there they came fringed and shredded by shot and shell, begrimed by smoke, and scorched by flame, but *wreathed with victory*—victory at last—and our poor heart broke down as those banners, baptized in blood, spoke from all their gaping wounds of the noble heroes who had borne them. Ah! they were *veterans!*

So, God calls for *men;* sun-browned and battle-scarred, inured to hardships and inspired by victory. The pure in heart and life are such. They have quivered in the hurtling fires of death, they have groped amid the smoke of conflict, they have crossed the cold glittering steel with old habits of the nature, they have swept in a rolling tide of victory through the fields of old indulgence, and they are to-day bearing in triumph the blood-stained banner of the cross. God's veterans are they! And they are recruiting their ranks for other campaigns and other victories.

It is said that the Turks inscribe upon their sword-blades the choicest sentences of their

Koran, in order that the most cherished sentiments of their faith may be found in closest proximity with the most effective blows. So, we would to-day inscribe upon our weapons, "Holiness to the Lord!" that our gleaming steel may flash our faith at every blow!

Sanctified men become conductors of Omnipotence.

When the will of God is accomplished in their sanctification, they are avenues through which its omnipotence reaches the world. We have heard believers complain of an almost agonizing sense of want. We have heard their groanings after power. We have felt them like inextinguishable yearnings drinking up the life. We have tried to analyze them, to trace them to their origin and find a remedy; and we declare to you to day —Christian of the longing soul—there is a resting place. You may lose those unutterable yearnings *in a calm consciousness of being God's instrument and working all his will!* Holiness is power! Purity is the enginery of Omnipotence! Spirit purity we have in regeneration. Habit purity we have in sanctification. Power purity we have when unbelief—the last old habit that dies the death—is extirpated. Those sanctified ones who groan for power need yet another sanctifying touch. Unbelief in its last lingering doubtings must be substituted by an all-embracing faith, and that will give the endowment of power!

"Ye shall receive power after that the Holy Ghost is come upon you."

Come, then, Mighty Sanctifier, and herald the baptism of power!

It needs only that your sanctified soul shall concentrate all its believing energies in one burning focus that shall fuse down and dissipate the last lingering unbelief of your nature. If you like the expression, "Lay it upon the altar!" If you prefer philosophical phraseology, *substitute faith for it*, and ye shall receive the power. But remember, inspiration is a mighty helper. Remember! The Holy Spirit can revolutionize a habit, with your concurring will and faith, in a single instant. Come then, just now, and begin the work. Holy Spirit, help! The sprinkled blood is nigh. The altar flame aspires. The sacrifice is bound. Old unbelief writhes in bonds. *Now,* High Priest above, we cast him on the fire! He groans, he dies! Faith lives, and claims, and triumphs now! All glory to the Lamb!

Now do not mistake, by supposing this endowment of power to be a certain consiousness that you are so filled with power, that it emanates from you, like sun-beams from the sun. Rather regard yourself as an *unobstructed conducting wire*, which needs only the connections to be instituted, in any Christian duty, and men are smitten with all the battery power of heaven.

Remember again. The lightning has its laws, and so has the Spirit of Omnipotence. Encased in glass, or robed in silk, the lightnings play around but do not flash upon you. So, the sovereignty of human will begirts men, and though God's Spirit may kindle convictions, it cannot always melt them into contrition or crystalize them into faith.

Your power will consist in this; *that whenever you discharge Christian duty, you do it so well that all that God can do for others, consistently with the laws of his moral government, will be done.* It will be manifest in a "*baptized persuasiveness*" that will subdue, and melt, and move, even though it fall, like the gentle sun-beam upon the icy cliffs of the mountain glacier. Tyndall tells us that a block of ice under the converged sun-beam, will suddenly (an inch, or inches below the surface) seem to resolve itself into a cluster of glittering stars, each with six petal-rays, shining with the luster of burnished silver.

Those petal-rays are a tiny water-flower, formed around a star-like vacuum, and vieing in beauty with the frost-works of a winter's morn. So, down deep in the icy heart of the worldling, the little water-flowers are forming round the vacuum that glitters in the consciousness, under the melting power of Love, and the little water drops trickle out here and there, when none but the All-Seeing notes their fall. Oh for the "*baptized persuasiveness*" of the Gospel! In the pulpit; in the altar; in the prayer-meeting; in the class-room; in the family; in the street; in the workshop; *everywhere* where icy hearts expose their rigid fronts to the melting sun-beams of God's Love!

But some fearful one perhaps is asking, "Suppose I do receive the baptism of power, and no good results follow, what must I think?"

A few years ago, a young engineer was being examined for graduation, when his examiner proposed the following question: "Suppose you have a steam-pump constructed for a ship under your own supervision, and know that every thing is in perfect working order, yet when you throw out the hose it will not draw. What would you think?"

"I should think, sir, there must be a defect some where."

"But such a conclusion is not admissible, for the supposition is that every thing is perfect, and yet it will not work."

"Then sir, I should look over the side to see if the river had run dry!"

So, in the case supposed—we should look out to see if God had vanished from the universe! Holiness is power! "There is in the Christian in whom the Lord dwells a conquering power also, that would be marvelous indeed if it did not belong to Him who dwelleth in the bush, and not to the Christian in himself at all. Moses was conquered before the bush in a few moments. He was virtually conquered when he stopped to look; for when he saw the bush that it burned and yet was not consumed, the impulse was masterly in him to see why it was. And when the voice came to him out of the midst of the bush, that was kingly, and he obeyed it. When it said "Draw not nigh hither," he obeyed. And when it said, "Put off thy shoes," he did so. Such a bush is the Christian in whom the Holy One dwells, and by whom he shines and speaks. There is in him, the Conquering One, with whom is all power on on earth and in heaven. The power is in the Christian, yet does not inhere in him. It is in the Christian because the Conquering One is in him, and the conquering power inheres in the Conquering One himself." (*W. E. Boardman* "*In the Power of the Spirit,*" etc.

"There was a pious lady who possessed this power. She was one of the weak things of this world. This power kept her unspotted from the world·

For fourteen years she was watched by an infidel who vainly endeavored to find some flaw in her daily life to strengthen him in his sceptical views. She was not aware of his intentions. Kept by this inward power of the Holy Spirit she walked on in the way, until at last the infidel was convicted by her godly, unassuming life, and brought to the feet of Jesus. This power is living and will be felt where it exists." *" The Living Epistle."*

When Christians, endowed with this power-purity, meet in prayer, the very atmosphere may be so pervaded by a supernatural Presence that men's consciousness shall recognize it on the instant, and they shall be constrained to say—"Lo, God is here!" "Ye shall receive power after that the Holy Ghost is come upon you." Come then Heavenly Anointing! Come Enshrining power! These vessels long for Thy filling! These lives await thy moulding.

Some illustrative examples, furnished by Rev. Dr. Asa Mahan in *" Divine Life,"* may help our faith.

" When attending a conference at Red Hill, some years since, a minister from Australia referred to a member of his own church, a young woman who labored as a domestic. On learning, after she had sought and obtained 'the promise of the Spirit,' that wages were very much higher in a distant part of the country than where she was, she went thither. The speaker then read a letter which he had just received from the pastor of the church where this young woman had gone. 'As I listened' said the writer, 'to the remarks of that young woman in the class and prayer-meetings one fact very deeply impressed my mind, namely, that *she was possessed of a power that I had not.* So deep did that impression at length become, that I went to her and requested her to tell me the secret of that new and divine life which she was living. In listening to her statements, I saw clearly my own deficiency and need, and sought and obtained an 'endument of power from on high.' The result of speaking to my people in the 'power of this endless life,' has been a total revolution in the state of my church, and the addition to its membership of between six and seven hundred converts from the world around, while the work of the Lord, with no indications of abatement, is still going forward from strength to strength.' What a new power was brought into that community by the coming of that female domestic, coming as she did 'in the power of the Spirit.' In the city of Darlington lives a young lady named Annie Fothergill. Personally, she is one of the most modest, reserved, and unobtrusive ladies we ever met with. 'Naturally,' she once remarked to us, 'I was ridiculously timid.' About five years since, she occupied the sphere of governess in a wealthy family in that city. After her conversion, she read 'The Baptism of the Holy Ghost,' sought and received 'the promise of the Spirit.' On receiving 'the anointing,' this passage was given to her as the fixed maxim of her life; namely, 'Whatsoever he saith to you, do it.' Under the influence of this, the will of Christ, whenever, and by whatsoever means, made known, has been and is the immutable law of all her activity.

'Soon after her endument of power,' while worshiping with her own people, the Friends, on the Sabbath, an opportunity presented itself in which it was manifestly proper for her to give public testimony to the power of Divine grace to which she had been subject. As soon as she thought of doing this, all the timidity of her nature arose, and rendered it seemingly impossible for her to speak at all. She at once lifted up her heart in silent prayer to Christ, that he would take all that fear away; give her perfect self-possession and readiness to speak or not to speak as he should will. In an instant this prayer was consciously answered, and this perfectly self-possessed readiness to act or speak for Christ, whenever and wherever duty requires, has never left her.

As soon as she became conscious that it was the will of Christ that she should speak, she arose and perfectly electrified the audience by her testimony. From that time a new era dawned upon that people. Soon after this, a lady, who had a large Bible-class of young women under her instruction in the Sabbath school, having occasion to be absent from the city for several weeks, requested Miss F. to take charge of her class during the interval. This, the latter, after prayer for Divine direction, consented to do. On her return, the teacher was surprised and delighted to find every one of her pupils 'rejoicing in hope of the glory of the Lord.'

At this time Miss F. received a request from the conductors of the Sabbath school to take charge of a band of about forty lads in the school, lads from 12 to 18 years of age, and so utterly lawless that they were called 'The Awkward Squad.' Finding it utterly impossible to preserve order among them, or in the school when they were present, their expulsion had been determined on. As a last resort, the request referred to was presented to Miss F. After reflection and prayer, she consented to undertake the work to which she was called. The first time she met the band, she held their fixed and almost breathless attention for a full hour. She then invited any who might desire religious conversation with her to call at her place at a certain hour the next Tuesday evening. One called and was hopefully converted. The next week more than half-a-dozen came, and all left rejoicing in God. Soon that whole 'Squad' was organized into a Praying Band of the most devout character. Through these young converts, others were called in, and her room was flooded with converts and inquirers.

A larger room being procured, she was requested to hold another meeting, on another evening, for young women. This was done with a like result. Then a children's meeting was appointed; and, lastly, one for the more elderly class. For four years and a half, these four weekly meetings have been held without interruption. The result has been, that in connection with these meetings, some five hundred or more souls have been converted, all but two or three of whom are now walking in the truth. Nor is there any indication of an abatement of the power of the work, the late meetings, as we are informed by a letter just received from Miss F., being as successful as former ones. She now gives her whole time to religious services, and is called in all directions to help forward the work of God, and everywhere the same power attends her, as at home. When helping in a conference at Nottingham we heard remarks to this effect in respect to her: 'There is something mysterious about that young woman. Her voice is feeble; her whole manner the most unassuming and simple conceivable. Yet, while she has great power in drawing believers toward the Higher Life, the impenitent seem to be powerless to resist truth as she presents it.' All who like her, are 'full of faith and of the Holy Ghost,' will not be just what she is. All such, however, will be endued with power to 'shine as lights in the world;' and to 'speak unto men to edification, and exhortation, and comfort.'"

"Take one other example. Rev. William Taylor, 'in the power of the Spirit,' spent, as he states, seven months among the Kaffirs of Africa, speaking to the people through an interpreter. During this period 'the missionaries,' he says, 'reported the conversion to God of 7,000 Kaffirs.' Nor did the work abate after he left. We recently read of one native minister there for example, who never addressed an audience without from two to twelve, or more, being converted. It is in this country that that aged female is going from village to village, and gathering souls by scores and hundreds into the kingdom of God. When will the Church of God come to understand wherein her great strength lies? How long will she suffer herself to be shorn of her strength by the great enemy of God and man?"

3. *The subject applied to the ministry.*

1. *As a source of personal and pulpit power.*

Upon this point let facts be our only arguments. Bishop Peck, in "*Central Idea,*" pp. 385-7, narrates the case of a friend in these words:

"My friend —— had been but a short time from college. He was a preacher—a scholar—a gentleman. He had been sent to a station in the midst of a wealthy community, where there were but few members of the church, and where moralists, infidels, and speculators combined to support him. He preached constantly, learnedly, and, we presume, faithfully. Months passed, and no indications of good appeared. We met him at a camp-meeting. Holiness was the great theme of the meeting. We loved the young man and sought an opportunity to converse with him. He felt that all was not right. He believed himself a Christian, and lived with a fixed purpose to obey and serve God. But there was a want of power in his preaching. He could say good things, but they did not cut. He seemed to himself to be preaching into the air. He often felt the conviction that he needed a deeper work of grace. He prayed, and wept, and tried, but as it seemed in vain, to rise; and still he had no such power with God as he felt belonged to his sacred profession. We were in a prayer-meeting when he uttered with earnestness, but not with much emotion, the prayer—'O Lord, sanctify my soul!'"

Then follows an account of his struggles and blessing, and the Bishop continues: "The meeting closed, and 'another spirit' was in our friend. He was humble, simple-hearted, and sweet as a child. But the power of Jehovah was in his preaching and his prayers. His hearers were amazed at the change in the preacher. The spirit of holiness burned and flamed out in every sermon. The word, like a two-edged, burnished, Jerusalem blade, cut its way to the hearts of the people. Brave men wept like children. Strong men bowed themselves under a might which they could not see. Infidels trembled and stood aghast before the divinity which spake in the words and appeared in the movements of the man! The work was powerful beyond all precedent in that vicinity. It swept like fire through that hitherto hardened and unbelieving community, bringing down infidel teachers, moralists, and scoffers indiscriminately, before the altar of God. Whole families were converted, the church was firmly established, they who were not a people had become a strong and conquering army of the Lord; and all—let no one dare to doubt it—by the baptism of fire, which, in answer to faith and prayer, had fallen upon the servant of God."

Were this a solitary example in the history of the ministry, it might be reasonably questioned whether the results attributed to his asserted experience did not really proceed from some other cause. But the facts show that similar results, to a greater or less extent, follow such experiences with sufficient uniformity to prove a *relation* of sequence. Nor should this be wondered at. Love-power and faith-power, culminating in Holy-Ghost-power, are the very means which God has chosen by which to advance his cause in the world. Holiness is love-power and faith-power in their mightiest subjective operations.

These forces *turned outward*, are co-operated with by Holy-Ghost-power just as spontaneously and instantaneously as the Holy Spirit works inwardly upon the establishment of the appropriate conditions. Hence, the more completely dominant these forces are in the heart's experience, **the more** thoroughly co-operative will the divine **Power** be in the objective work! This is simply the philosophy of the fitness of things! Moreover it is in perfect harmony with God's announced principle of gospel work, namely: "That the excellency of the power may be of God and not of men." Therefore the less of self, and the more of Christ, the less of "roots of bitterness," and the more of "holiness," must of necessity result in more of gospel fruits.

The types of the old dispensation had a most significant bearing upon this very point. The scrupulous care which priests were bound to exercise in the performance of their functions, to keep themselves ceremonially *clean*, was undoubtedly designed to impress Israel with the fact that Jehovah was a God of purity, and that those who stood between Him and the people should be correspondingly without spot. Hence, "Be ye clean that bear the vessels of the Lord," was recognized, not only as a proper ritualistic command, but as expressing an imperative demand arising from the necessities of the case. That was a time of shadows. The morning had not then dawned. But the "fullness of time" came. The gospel sun blazed out God's purity in effulgence brighter far than Horeb's fire-crowned summit or tabernacle or temple "glory." And with the growing radiance God's commissions widened, his empowerments multiplied and augmented, his agencies changed from the outward and visible to the inward and "not carnal," and a deeper spirituality and more satisfying communion became the marked and prominent characteristics of the dispensation of the Spirit!

That *heart-purity* and *faith-power* should *now* be the *measure* of *ministerial efficiency*, can surely not be deemed out of keeping with the design and spirit of this new dispensation. The Jewish priest must be pure externally, in a system of externals; the Christian minister must be pure internally, in a system of internals. God's Power preserved his people then. His Grace preserves his people now. "The sword of the Lord and of Gideon" gained conquests then. "My Spirit, saith the Lord," and "the words of their testimony," win triumphs now. Hence an experience molded by the Holy Spirit, a heart in restful reliance upon the promise, "I am with thee," a faith claiming all of aggressive efficiency that God can bring out of the natures under sway— these are the prime conditions of successful labor. That they are furnished in larger measure and less counterpoised by an experience of heart purity than by one of heart impurity, is too evident to need argument.

Behold, then, the tremendous responsibility of the true minister of Christ! He is not only to preach what he believes to be the truth, but such practical truth as will touch human nature at all points of its contact with sin; and *so* to preach such truth, as to make it evident that he is not theorizing but *testifying*, and testifying not merely a gospel antagonism to some sins, but a gracious extirpation of all voluntary sins. Here he exemplifies a boundlessness that honors God's grace, and an exclusiveness that is in perfect correspondence with His purity, instead of being a practical apologist for man's infirmities, and a special pleader for life-long carnality.

Men who buy goods "by sample" judge of the quality of the stock by the samples shown. Ministers are most emphatically *sample exhibitors* to the world. The honor of the house and the prospects of trade depend upon the right selection and faithful exhibition. Therefore, every Christian minister's preaching should be, in substance, "I declare unto you that which I do know;" and his knowledge should be deep enough and broad enough to furnish a fair sample of what grace can do to save a sinner from guilt, and self, and habits of perversion. *Then*, God can use him, and take the glory of results to *himself*. "That the excellency of the power may be of God and not of man."

This experience is the focalization of every human instrumentality and consequent securement of the maximum of divine co-operative power. This focalization is the one-ideaism of an all-commanding purpose; the constraining magnetism of a mighty assurance; the electrifying enthusiasm of a faith that asks without doubting, trusts without fearing and works without wearying—accompanied by a self-surrender that ignores the prudence of selfishness, and deems crosses and perils things to profit by, thus exhibiting a zeal that inflames under difficulties and is inspired by obstacles to a more consuming fervor, and an eager watchfulness that stands ready girded upon the outposts of past conquest listening for the call of duty in every opening opportunity, while yearning with unappeasable soul-hunger to see men saved, and groaning out importunate entreaties in the unutterable beseechings of Gethsemanes of Christly sympathy.

Another consideration is presented by Bishop E. L. Janes in "*Perfect Love,*" p. 18. "Christian holiness invests the gospel minister with the power of usefulness in the time of advanced years. The time is coming when . . . by the pressure of years and infirmities, we shall be obliged to retire from the active work of the ministry. Such will find holiness of heart and life the best substitute for the activities of the ministry."

278   CHRISTIAN HOLINESS.

2. *As a means of revival interest.*

Revivals are largly special results of the opera tion of religious sympathies. Some Christian deep ly imbued with a sense of the peril of his unsaved friends, wrestles in prayer for their salvation. As his mind is wrought up in the exercise into increased ardor, the sympathetic element glows with more intense fervor. By the law of the Spirit's action his operations are correspondingly increased both upon the hearts of the subjects of prayer, and upon those whose spirits are in fellowship with the praying one. These catch the influence and widen the circle of special sympathy and corresponding effort and a revival is the result.

Now, if we inquire what quality in the experience of Christians best fits them to be in a state of spontaneous sympathy with those who may be deeply exercised for the salvation of the impenitent, the answer must be—There are but two qualities supposable, namely, (1) Mixed carnality and purity, or, (2) Christian purity. Between the two it would be an impeachment of ordinary intelligence to suppose that any one could hesitate for a moment.

If wilful blindness should still insist that it is de- debatable ground, one preliminary question should be settled before the debate begins, namely : what is the causal connection between carnality and Christian sympathy? When that is definitely decided as within the realm of favoring possibilities, then indeed may Christain sympathy be supposed to be the fruit of unchrisitan tendencies, enmities may generate friendships, sin may help holiness.

Crowding the investigation a little further back, it needs but a moment's consideration to show that the same quality which best fits Christians to imbibe this spirit of earnest prayerful sympathy from others, likewise best prepares them to become the *root springs* of such sympathy. Hence it follows, that whether we seek for the best heart-preparation for becoming a first nucleus of revival energy, or re-inforcements to such energy already in the struggle, in either case heart purity has the *maximum of constitutional spontaneities, and the minimum of clogging antagonisms.*

The essential quality of such experience therefore, commends it as a means of revival interest. The possibilities of such an experience are open to every believer; therefore, within every believer inhere the potential factors of a revival. That is, heart-purity realized, and its loving sympathies actualized in special work, the revival spirit as naturally ensues as heat from a flame. "A man who is filled with the *efficiency* which is of God, has a revival within him, and it must develop. There is about him the swing of victory."

How vast then must be the responsibility of those who decline, or neglect the empowerment for lack of which Zion languishes and the world dies! Nor can any of the ordinary excuses palliate the guilt of such neglect. Our mission is not to plead exemption, but to be saving men and women; not to beg for indulgences, but to represent our self-sacrificing Lord; not to trim to worldly maxims and shape our course by self-seeking principles, but to be dead to the world and to crucify self. If we are animated by this spirit, we shall not quibble over terms and strive to see how little holiness is compatible with a Christian profession, but abandoning ourselves to the spirit-quickened instincts of our regenerated hearts, we shall feel best satisfied in getting farthest from the world, and most in our native element when giving loving sympathies full play.

A Church exhibiting these preferences is, *by the very necessities of the case* IN revival work, so long as they thus continue. On the contrary. who does not know that the most important and the most difficult work of preparation for revivals consist in labored attempts to extirpate the carnal tastes, dissipations, and habits of professed

Christians? To ministers, therefore, as leaders in the revival movements of the church, God has a right to look for the best attainable personal experience to fit them for their position. "Like priest, like people," contains an intimation of responsibility of tremendous significance in this connection.

4. *The subject applied to the Press.*
1. As a standard of public morality.

One of the mightiest forces of modern civilization is *The Press*—that multiform potency which interpenetrates the family, society, business circles, political associations, national councils, and international assemblies; and before which the peasant in his hamlet, and the king upon his throne, alike bow in deference. That such a force should have not only a correct but *the best standard of public morality*, is a matter of immense importance to the public weal. As it now is—divided against itself —its utterances as a whole have not the clear ring of the most high-toned principle, and therefore fail to prove the boon to humanity that good men have a right to expect.

There is a gospel of purity in the world, enshrined in the Sacred Book, whose divine truths have lifted modern civilization from the semi-barbarism of the past, and that can guide men amid all the intricacies of ambitious state-craft, and all the whirls of political intrigue, and all the perplexities of clashing business enterprises, and by their very exclusiveness in supreme excellence, these truths demand the recognition of the intelligence of the world—such recognition as can be given only by the elevation of the principle of Christian purity to the place of the *ultimate standard* in practical morality.

2. As a reformatory agency among men.

Let that standard be adopted in all editorial sanctums as the " unabridged" authority upon all ethical questions, and the mists of doubt that hang like portents of disaster over so many social customs, business expedients and political policies, would dissolve like the fogs of the morning; public sentiment—that wizened specter of compromise —that feared and hated, cajoled and outraged reality—would walk the earth as an evangel of purity and peace. Let this standard be adopted, and the "line upon line and precept upon precept," with which the press would deluge society, would do more than furnish a practical standard of right living, for these efforts to *guide* the virtuous masses would in the very nature of things give an upward trend to all social stratas, and prove *reformatory* by just so much as they are elevating. All reformation does not consist in snatching individuals from special careers of crime; indeed the very best is that which takes hold of viciously disposed blood and brain, and by added impulses toward right, or change of environments, modifies or neutralizes the virus, and renders the product something other than criminal. That a sanctified press would furnish such impulses and help to change the surroundings of the unfortunate classes, cannot be questioned. The herding iniquities of over-crowded tenement house life, the festering sores of public dens of infamy, the licensed fever spots of alcoholic degradation —all these could be scathed and blighted out of being by the burning words of rebuke that a holy press might shower upon them like indignant heaven's fires upon their prototype—the Sodom of old. And with the banishment of these potent pestilence breeders from social life would come, by legitimate substitution, something more in accord with purified public sentiment and vastly more helpful to the wretched victims of inborn vicious tendencies, and equally encouraging to those who —under the teachings of the press—would be struggling to emancipate themselves from the thraldom of degrading habits. Thus would reformation stretch her hands of helpfulness to all imploring ones, while lifting the bed level of all unfavorable social life to such a plain as would render the process of childhood education something other than increasing capacity for and delight in the practices of evil.

The magnitude of the aggregate responsibility of the press can be measured only by the stupendous possibilities viewed in contrast with facts as they are. And the responsibility of the reader can only be estimated by the might of that *door opening* hand of Providence, which Paul instructed his converts to move by the power of their prayers. Col. 4 : 3. Let the Churches make prayer unto God without ceasing for the sanctification of the press.

5. *The subject applied to Institutions of Learning.*

1. As crowning culture with the glory of purity.

Character is the flower of being. Culture is a method of development. Development reaches its highest point of excellence in the most complete and perfect character.

The culture of a single faculty or set of faculties to the neglect of the complemental or counterpoising faculties, can end only in the unbalanced condition which is practical perversion. The intelectual and the esthetical may be developed to the highest degree, and the institutions in which the process is conducted will still be only nurseries of philosophical speculation, scientific research, and literary proficiency—not educators of the entire man. The moral and religious may be added, and still education may fall short of the high demands of a character-culture befitting those who aim to reach the maximum of human attainment.

Now add the spiritual power of personal sanctity to the embracing and interpenetrating atmosphere of college life, to the routine of chapel exercises, to the personal magnetism of social and official intercourse, and to the authoritative interpretations of truth in the recitation and lecture rooms, and it will need no theological addenda to the curriculum to cause the rays that gild the homes of culture to brighten to a golden glory like that whose splendors enfolded the burnished roof of Jerusalem's Temple in the full effulgence of the eastern sun.

2. As approximating the attainable perfection of manhood.

Following the analogy suggested by the more and more upright successive forms of the vertabrate type of animal life—fishes, reptiles, birds, and mammals—the conclusion has been reached upon purely scientific ground, that the coronal is the crowning development of creation, (See Agassiz, Dana, and others.) Physio-psychology has demonstrated that the coronal is the special physical instrument of the moral and religious. Therefore it seems strictly philosophical to infer that man approximates his highest attainable perfection in the complete sovereignty of the coronal over the basilar—in other words, of the spiritual over the animal. If this proposition be accepted, it follows that the experience which is most purely spiritual, i. e., least dominated or influenced by the carnal is the nearest to the ideal that we must entertain of the perfect man.

That this is in exact accordance with the design of the Gospel is evident in such passages as this: "That the man of God may be *perfect*, thoroughly furnished unto all good works." That *this* perfection has an element of the supernatural does not in the least detract from its desirableness. On the other hand, none know so well as the scholars within, or made by the institutions of learning, how all the ages testified to man's moral impotency unaided by something out of or above himself. And none should be so quick as these men of culture to detect the fact that the keenest science may find its ultimate in the very supernatural which supplements man's best endeavors to reach an ideal perfection, with a co-efficiency that realizes at length "the measure of the stature of the fullness of Christ."

3. As giving such institutions the moulding power that they ought to possess.

To say that that power must be anything less than the culture of the entire man after the best and most vigorous type of development, is to say that humanity has not yet evolved institutions commensurate with its needs or representative of its aspirations. We are unwilling to charge such deficiency upon the honored seats of learning which have been esteemed hitherto as the well-ripened fruit of human progress. And if they have in the past largely delegated special spiritual culture to the church, let it not be construed as the abnegation of a right to lay their plastic hand upon the highest destinies of men, but rather as an indication of voluntary devotion to the comparatively inferior interest of mental training.

If our philosophy be correct—not as an exposition of a dogma, but as an explanation of a *fact* —then is that fact demonstrated; and the demonstration of an experimental fact necessarily throws it within the catalogue of some department of science; and as one prime object of colleges and universities is to teach and illustrate science, therefore, whatever moral or religious power they can wield by the scientific and practical presentation of the great fact of holiness of heart is a measure of influence that legitimately pertains to their sphere.

It should be matter of profound gratitude that there are institntions of learning which dare to make prominent, as the acme of human culture a Christly Spiritual perfection engrafted upon and the outgrowth of a symmetrical and complete mental development, sustained by a vigorous and unperverted physical organism. May the day soon dawn that shall see *all* arrayed in a line of sanctified effort that shall fill the sphere of responsibility, bless men, and glorify God with the ripened fruits of human progress allied with transforming grace. Amen.

THE POWER OF GRACE

OVER ACQUIRED HABITS, SPECIAL INBORN PERVERSITIES, AND THE NATURAL APPETITES,

TO WHICH IS ADDED

"THE WONDROUS NAME,"

By Rev. S. H. PLATT, A. M.,

Exhibiting the Power of Grace in the complete breaking up of established Habits, and the *instantaneous extirpation* of Appetites that have held sway for years.

The *Tobacco, Opium, Rum* and *Sexual* Appetites, and the *Habits* of Irritability and Gluttony, are treated from the standpoint of actual experience.

Full of facts and illustrative examples which ministers can use.

"Its details of marvelous triumphs over appetite, are full of inspiration to *special workers*, such as Crusaders, Praying Bands, Young Men's Christian Associations, and others."

"It inspires hope in bosoms that have long ceased to hope."

"*Every victim of perverse appetite or evil habit, and every friend of such victim*, should read this book."

The works from the pen of this gifted and talented preacher of the gospel are all so full of life and spiritual power, that it only needs to announce the issue of a new book from him, to secure for it the widest circulation. The present little work, very handsomely gotten up by the publisher, is well worthy of taking a place by the side of the author's other productions, such as "Princely Manhood," "Elijah the Tishbite," "The Philosophy of Christian Holiness," &c., and should be carefully studied by all over whom the power of evil habits has been exercised. In it science and religion are united to form a philosophy, ample enough to meet every case, and, if carried into practice, to break down the power of reigning sin, and the besetments of our nature.—*The Christian Visitor.*

Most useful, valuable and instructive. Should it have a circulation commensurate with its merits, it would be read by all. It strikes at the very root of evil. It is logical, powerful and convincing, and clothed with such elegance of diction and beauty of expression that the appreciative reader cannot well close the book till he has finished it. It abounds in beautiful passages, but pages 167-8 are the most sublime, beautiful and poetical that we have ever read.—*The Well Spring.*

Is well written, and the author is a man of learning and ability.—*Pittsburgh Christian Advocate.*

Good people will rejoice with those whose experience the author adduces in proof of his theory.—*The Christian Union.*

Furnishes thoughtful and consolatory answers to all who inquire sincerely for salvation from sinful habits and evil appetites of all kinds.—*Pacific Christian Advocate.*

It is the most complete setting forth of the power of divine grace to save from acquired habits, special inborn perversities and the natural appetites, that has ever been published in this country.—*Christian Standard and Home Journal.*

This is a timely and forcible effort to show the practical power of faith in the control of the various forms of the self-life included in the title. The argument is cumulative and powerful; the spirit kind and sympathetic; discriminations clear; inspirations strong and helpful. It is greatly needed, and it meets the want.—*Union in Christ.*

It displays much care and research.—*Brooklyn Eagle.*

It displays ripe scholarship.—*Brooklyn Argus.*

Rev. S. H. Platt, A. M., of Brooklyn, has done the cause of truth great service in the issue of this little work and to which he has added his great sermon on the "Wondrous Name."

Mr. Platt is mentally given to analysis, and has been led to close research in natural philosophy. The little book before us is the answer to the following questions in brief: 1. Can grace, under nervous exhaustion, maintain in us a freedom from irritability? 2. Is *felt* irritability of temper inconsistent with a holy heart? 3. Can we be instantaneously delivered from the power of *acquired* habit? 4. May we expect deliverance from *inborn* cravings for stimulants, &c., in answer to prayer for purifying grace? 5. Can the strongest appetite of the human organism be so subdued in a moment by the power of the

Holy Spirit, that thereafter, solicitation to indulgence shall not disturb the peace of the soul? 6. May we hope that we may be freed from matured inherent perversity, so that we may thereafter rest from frequent or almost constantly soul-harrassing conflict with desire? Having in a somewhat more elaborate manner than we have given them stated his queries, Mr. Platt proceeds by the direct method of answer, of—"to the law and to the testimony;" "in the mouth of two or three witnesses shall every word be established."

First selecting the tobacco habit, as a representative of its class, and furnishing a fearful array of evidence of its destructive effects, and instancing cases of earnest and most hopeless struggles with the dominant evil, Mr. Platt boldly declares of all efforts at reform: " Instantaneous extirpatation, by the power of grace, in answer to prayer is the best way." "Is it possible? Let testimony decide." Then under their appropriate headings the author gives the result of close reading and extensive correspondence on the subject, which conclusively proves that there is no habit, however confirmed, which may not be instantaneously eradicated by the power of the Holy Ghost. The instances of the thorough eradication of long acquired sinful indulgences are numerous and startling enough to create hope in the bosom of the most despairing, and conclusive enough to stop the mouth of every gainsayer.

The sermon which follows is really but a development of the great question of the author's book—"Is grace Almighty?" The pleasing and confidential style of the preacher wins the attention of his reader from the first, while the strangely unconscious incisiveness of the practical questions advanced makes every one feel that "there is something here for me!" We confess that it is a long time since we have risen from the perusal of a sermon which, beside the great subject on which it treats, has so impressed us with its practicability and beauty as this sermon on "The Wondrous Name."—*The Christian Standard.*

FOURTH EDITION.

Muslin, 16 v o., 185 pages, printed on fine tinted and calendered paper, and sent post paid, for 80c. to any address; same with Photo. of the author, 90c.; flexible cloth edition, 40c.

THE HOPE PUBLISHING CO.,
9 DE BEVOISE PLACE, BROOKLYN, N. Y

PRINCELY MANHOOD:

A Private Treatise

ON THE PROCREATIVE INSTINCT AS RELATED TO MORAL AND CHRISTIAN LIFE.

FOR MALES ONLY.

By Rev. S. H. PLATT, A. M.

EIGHTH EDITION.

What is said about " Princely Manhood:"

It is clear, earnest and pure. I trust it meets a large sale. Its entire freedom from mercenary and other unworthy motives, gives it a strong claim upon the attention of parents. I do not see why you should say, "for adults only." I should be more than willing to have a daughter or son of ten or twelve years of age read and study every line of it. Hoping that you will use every honorable means to secure a broad distribution of this admirable little work, I am, Yours very truly,

Dio Lewis.

The main purpose of this writing is to thank you for "Princely Manhood," a copy of which I saw yesterday for the first time. I have read it through twice. I am forty-six years old, have read many books and more men, but in this little book now for the first time have seen a plain statement of a truth I have known to exist. This generation will die unsaved, but the time will come when good men will understand and obey this truth that you have so modestly set forth. *I know how much need there is of it, and could write a volume of illustrative facts to prove its necessity.*

A Prominent Business Man of Brooklyn.

We advise parents to read this book.

Mrs. Annie Wittenmeyer.

"I shall feel it my duty, as a Christian minister, to circulate Princely Manhood. * * * It will do a vast amount of good."
—A widely-known Clergyman in the West.

A gentleman in high official position, in Brooklyn, N. Y., writes:

"Acquaintance with its truths will be of inestimable value to all who seek high moral or Christian attainments. It is a scientific, philosophical and Christainly showing of matters most intimately connected with human welfare, and of which most are deplorably ignorant."

From Brooklyn also comes the following indorsement by one of its most successful physicians:

"The theme is one that has been thought to belong only to my own profession, yet I see no objection to its careful handling by any prudent minister who is sufficiently acquainted with the related sciences to speak intelligently about it. Mr. Platt's treatment of the subject is thoroughly scientific, intensely practical, chaste in expression, and, in its exhibition of the helpfulness of Grace, greatly exalting to one's conception of the Gospel as a Cure for human sin. It will not *only* do *good*, but just the *kind* of good most *needed*."

Another intelligent and successful physician writes from a city in Connecticut:

"Its influence for good upon the lives and health of those who read it can scarcely be estimated. I believe it will harmonize many domestic difficulties, and so instruct parents that children will be saved from many pernicious habits."

A clergyman, of Boston, says: "It ought to be read by every adult in the world."

"Its statements are so clear, its conclusions so sound, its spirit so pure and exalted, that I would fully recommend it to all the world."

Another, in New Haven, writes:

"It is a mighty incentive to true, royal Christian manhood."

The president of a Southern college writes:

"Other books of great value have been written upon this subject, and many more will be, and, on account of the immense importance thereof, need be. Some of these I have read, and none of them without seeing in them excellencies. Your work, however, *exceeds them all in this, that it looks at the subject from the standpoint of exalted spiritual life.* When you so strongly present the blessings of ' *the sanctified disuse* of any faculty or function which Providence bars out of legitimate opportunity,' you lay open one of the noblest manifestations of a true faith in God and obedience to Him. A volume might be evolved from the broad truth here opened.

"It is well said that purity of thought is the most difficult attainment in the Christian life, and the author, in his attempt to elevate the struggling aspirant to a life of rectitude, has evinced a brave indifference to prurient sensibilities, and a noble aim to benefit humanity. We could wish that this outspoken, honest, and convincing book might go forth, not only to correct existing evils, but prevent the demoralization caused by such infamous literature as tends only to inflame passion and ruin body and soul."—METHODIST HOME JOURNAL.

"Except the Bible, no father can give his child a more valuable literary keepsake than this. Millions of money and years of life would be saved if men would heed its words."—A PROFESSIONAL WRITER.

"It must do much good and is greatly needed."—Rev. E. P. HAMMOND (the Evangelist).

A gentleman connected with the Associated Press of New York writes: Dear Mr. Platt:—In acknowledging the receipt of your unequaled book on "Princely Manhood," let me thank you for the soul feast I had in reading it. You have given, in my judgment, the only *practical* solution of this much vexed question. Could I but have read this work years ago it would have shed much light on a dark pathway. I never supposed that *from temptation you would evolve strength to resist temptation.* This you have substantially done. The more I think of it the stranger it seems to me that ministers of the gospel should so long have held their peace. This I can only regard as reprehensible in the extreme. *Where the most light is needed, there we find utter darkness.* The subject is mainly handled *from mercenary* motives by quacks and charlatans, who, with their illustrated works, but pour gunpowder into a magazine already on fire.

I shall take great pains to circulate this work and have already called attention to it through the press. Were I able I would place it in the hands of every young man competent to receive the truth and bid him find therein the firm yet gentle guidance his wavering soul is longing for.

If your Queenly Womanhood is half as ably gotten up, I think you owe it to a suffering generation to place it in their hands as speedily as possible."

"Princely Manhood is a peculiar volume, treating in a singularly delicate and healthful way a most difficult and tender theme. It is a d., cussion of the sexes and their most sacred relations from the standpoint of a living, holy Christian experience. We welcome the book, and wish it a wide reading in this wicked age."—*Sunday School Teachers Journal.*

"I am very much pleased with "Princely Manhood," and wish I could have possessed it years ago. I have always felt that there was too much false modesty in refraining from treating such subjects in a Scriptural manner."—*Rev. John Q. Adams.*

"'Princely Manhood' is truly a book for the times, and of great value."—*The World's Crisis.*

"A valuable book."—*A Prominent Presiding Elder of Ohio.*

"I consider Princely Manhood the best of its kind." "Ought to be in every mans's hand."—*An influential Minister of New Jersey.*

"You have intrepidly and wisely treated a subject—'Princely Manhood'—on which information is much needed, and one which it is almost impossible to treat orally, as you have so faithfully and successfully done with the pen.—*C. K. True, D. D.*

"Allow a layman to thank you for Princely Manhood." Had it been placed in my hands earlier in life I would be to-day a stronger and better man. It is one of the most valuable books that I ever read. *One of the best known Business Men of Brooklyn.*

"I have read many works on anatomy, the sexual function and its abuse, &c., but have failed to find one which treated the subject from the stand point you have done. This is the true position, though almost entirely ignored by medical writers. It should be read carefully by parents especially that they may realize the danger of leaving their children in ignorance."—*A Wealthy Business Man.*

"Princely Manhood" and "Queenly Womanhood" have been recommended to me very highly by Rev. G. P., M. D. of this place. *A Clergyman of Conn.*

"A most excellent work and I trust you may increase its circulation a hundred fold."—*A Lay Delegate to the General Conference.*

A full Index of Princely Manhood will be sent free to any address. 16mo, 156 pages. Sent post-paid, paper, 50 cents; cloth, 60 cents, by

THE HOPE PUBLISHING CO.,

9 DE BEVOISE PLACE, BROOKLYN, N. Y.

If the price seems high, it should be remembered that all *special works* are necessarily so; but this is FAR BELOW *the average of special works.*

QUEENLY WOMANHOOD:

A Private Treatise,

FOR FEMALES,

ON THE SEXUAL INSTINCT AS RELATED TO MORAL AND RELIGIOUS LIFE.

By Rev. S. H. PLATT, A. M.

FOURTH EDITION.

This work is the *complement* of Princely Manhood, and has for the female sex the same delicate statement of facts, a like clearness of theory, and the same presentation of the glorious *possibilities* that have rendered Princely Manhood an unequaled counsellor and help to males.

IT IS A BOOK FOR EVERY MOTHER, WIFE AND DAUGHTER.

Says the Author: "From the numerous revelations made to us in the course of thirty years of the most confidential relations with people in all the walks of life, we are prepared to affirm that were 'Princely Manhood' and 'Queenly Womanhood' made a part of the home reading of every boy and girl in the land, multitudes would be saved from *habits*, the injurious character of which they do not know, and the *fact* of which their parents do not suspect; and multitudes of the after marriage estrangements—culminating in divorce courts, the mutual separations, and the chronic home repellances (worse even than separation)—would never occur."

What is said of "Queenly Womanhood:"

"I have received one copy of "Queenly Womanhood," but it is so *good* and *true* that I cannot keep it at home. It is twenty miles away now, and I want another."—*Mrs. F——, of A——, Mich.*

Rev. S. H. Platt, A. M., is the well-known Methodist clergyman whose healing by the prayer of faith, at Brooklyn, N. Y., several years since, excited much attention and comment. He is a man of marked ability, originality and power; one for whom great things have been done by the divine Master. He is the author of "Princely Manhood," and "Queenly Womanhood," two volumes peculiar in their kind, but of much value to those for whom they are intended. Doubtless the author is right in his facts, advice and conclusions. It is well for m[en] and women to read and ponder these volumes. They will learn thin[gs] they knew not, learn the terrible power of temptation, learn swe[et] charity, learn how weak they all are, learn the power of grace and ho[w] strong they may become in Jesus Christ.—*The Bible Banner.*

"Having received great help from the perusal of your works (Princ[e]ly Manhood and Queenly Womanhood), I can do no less than thar[k] you most heartily for the good words they contain, and wish every m[an] and woman, boy and girl might read them. They have been of unto[ld] value to me."—*F. A. Z. of Conn.*

"I desire a supply of your private works, Princely Manhood a[nd] Queenly Womanhood, for circulation in India. I am sure they a[re] greatly needed and I think their circulation will do good."—*W. J. G[.], Bombay, India.*

"I can think of no works so important in the exaltation of humani[ty] as your "Princely Manhood" and "Queenly Womanhood." I ha[ve] felt the need of them so much in my professions (physician and mini[s]ter), when I have met with so many who were suffering soul and bod[y] from ignorance of what they might learn, yet in the present state of s[o]ciety I could not communicate in conversation."—*Rev. A. N. H., M. D[.] of Mass.*

"Queenly Womanhood" and "The Power of Grace" are excelle[nt] works and should be more widely known and read."—*L. W. G., a pro[m]inent Official of Ontario, Canada.*

"Princely Manhood has done me untold good, for which I am ve[ry] grateful, and I desire "Queenly Womanhood," hoping it will do me [as] much good as its complement."—*C. C., of Conn.*

In the statement of general principles and such conclusions as rela[te] alike to *both sexes*, the matter is the same as "Princely Manhood[,]" while information for *females only* is found in "Queenly Womanhood" alone.

A full Index of "Queenly Womanhood" will be sent free to any address.

Fourth edition. 16mo., pp. 160, 60 cts., paper, 50 cts., post paid to any a[d]dress by

THE HOPE PUBLISHING CO.,

9 DE BEVOISE PLACE, BROOKLYN, N. Y[.]

MY TWENTY-FIFTH YEAR JUBILEE:

OR,

CURE BY FAITH AFTER TWENTY-FIVE YEARS OF LAMENESS.

By Rev. S. H. PLATT, A. M.

A plain statement of the permanent cure of the Author from a lameness of twenty-five years' standing, *by no other means than* FAITH IN PRAYER.

"We admit the high character of Mr. Platt and the entire reliability of any facts stated by him."—*N. Y. Witness.*

"He is well known, and the cure is well authenticated. Why should we marvel?"—*Baptist Union.*

"Is this a miracle or is it not? If not, what is it?"—*Christian at Work.*

"God is increasing the faith of his people, giving more and more reliance upon Him to heal the souls and bodies of men in answer to believing prayers. Lord, increase our faith." "Why should not the prayer-force be able to produce results as tangible as any other force in the universe?"—*New York Herald.*

"We trust that we may hear of many thousands of such cures."—*Newark Daily Advertiser.*

"Personal knowledge of the author increases our confidence in his remarkable story."—*The Advance.*

"My Twenty-fifth Year Jubilee is wonderfully encouraging to faith in God's promises."—*Union in Christ.*

12mo, 60 pp. Sent post paid to any address for 15 cents. ENLARGED EDITION, containing reply to critics, 20 cents.

THE HOPE PUBLISHING CO.,

9 DE BEVOISE PLACE, BROOKLYN, N. Y.

THE MAN OF LIKE PASSIONS:

OR,

ELIJAH THE TISHBITE.

By Rev. S. H. PLATT, A. M.

THIRD EDITION.

"Its character and scope are thus set forth in the preface:

"'A holy character impressively *pictured* to the mind becomes treasure in the memory, and a formative power in the experience. T grandest life in ancient history was that of the Tishbite Prophet, a these pages strive to bring it, as in panoramic vision, before the observe

"We think every reader will pronounce the work a fulfillment of t purpose thus announced."—*Winsted Herald.*

It is a *pen portrait* of that MAN OF FIRE, drawn in colors vivid as t lightnings of his mountain home, and revealing the SOURCES of l POWER, and the GLORY of his CHARACTER.

Its practical lessons, glowing with pious ardor, are a MIGHTY INSPI ATION toward the noblest type of manhood, and the loftiest ideal Christian excellence. I read it this forenoon. A royal feast I ha food from the King's table. It made me pray, sing and rejoice. bless God for the dear little book. Oh that everybody could read —*Wm. Hauser, M. D.*

A critic, charmed with its style, has pronounced it "A PROSE POEM

Third edition, 16mo, 72 pp. Paper, 10 cents; cloth, 15 cents.

THE HOPE PUBLISHING CO.,

9 DE BEVOISE PLACE BROOKLYN, N.

NEVERTHELESS:

A Sermon.

By Rev. S. H. PLATT, A. M.

AT THE M. E. TABERNACLE, BROOKLYN, N. Y.,
JANUARY 13, 1878.

Dealing with some of the darker aspects of God's Providence in human life, it shows the alleviations that the Gospel presents.

A cheering, helpful, consolatory production, in the best style of the author.

The shadows and the sunshine, the sorrows and the joys are here so grouped that the beauty, grandeur and glory of God's plan stand out in doubt-silencing, wonder-wakening revealment. Send it to some sick or troubled friend. It will "do him good and not evil all the days of his life."

12mo, 30 pp. Six cents.

THE HOPE PUBLISHING CO.,

9 DE BEVOISE PLACE, BROOKLYN, N. Y.

THE WONDROUS NAME:

A Sermon,

By Rev. S. H. PLATT, A. M.

PREACHED AT THE MESSIAH CAMP MEETING, MILFORD, CONN., AUGUST 15, 1873.

"The pleasing and confidential style of the preacher wins the att[en-]tion of his reader from the first, while the strangely unconscious in[per-]siveness of the practical questions advanced makes everyone feel t[hat] 'there is something here for me!' We confess that it is a long ti[me] since we have risen from the perusal of a sermon which, besides [the] great subject on which it treats, has so impressed us with its practi[ca-]bility and beauty as this sermon on 'The Wondrous Name.'"—[*The*] *Christian Standard.*

"It abounds in beautiful passages, but pages 10-11 are the most s[ub-]lime, beautiful and poetical that I have ever read."—*Dr. I. Wins[low] Ayer, Editor of The Well Spring.*

"Beautiful!" "Grand!" "Glorious!" are some of the comm[on] expressions of readers as they close its pages. Ministers sometin[mes] read it to their congregations. It is helpful and soul-lifting to a rare [de-]gree. Order it for some tempted, troubled or afflicted friend. Sen[d it] to some son or daughter of poverty, struggling to keep the wolf fr[om] the door. It will nerve heart and arm together.

Eighth edition, 12mo, 33 pp. Six cents.

THE HOPE PUBLISHING CO.,
9 DE BEVOISE PLACE, BROOKLYN, N.[Y.]

THE PHILOSOPHY OF CHRISTIAN HOLINESS.

Originally published as a 24mo pamphlet, sermon (now out of print) is republished as a Treatise under the Title of

CHRISTIAN HOLINESS,

ITS

PHILOSOPHY, THEORY AND EXPERIENCE.

What was said of the Sermon:

Bishop R. S. Foster, D.D., LL.D., wrote: "It contains not only important and astutely expressed truth but, more than that, points the way to some deep and occult cases which are of real value to the discussion."

"I am pleased with its fresh and original way of treatment. Although novel it is essentially sound."—*James Strong, S. T. D.*

"This discourse by Rev. S. H. PLATT, from 1 Thess., iv. 3, for its originality and clear reasoning, and at the same time deep pathos and spiritual power, we have rarely heard equaled. We understand that at the spontaneous request of the preachers, and many interested hearers, the discourse is likely to be published. If it is, we bespeak for it a warm reception."—*Christian Advocate and Journal.*

"FRIDAY.—The stillness of that glorious morning in the woods, and the large attendance of glowing worshipers, with hearts and faces all radiant with the hallowed influence of a love-feast (in which forty-eight out of one hundred and twenty speakers testified to having received the sanctifying graces of the Holy Spirit), were improved by a sermon from Rev. S. H. PLATT, of Winsted, on the subject of sanctification, from 1 Thess., 4 : 3. Mr. PLATT'S well earned reputation of an independent thinker made all anticipate something fresh on a subject which, more than all others, perhaps, of a directly practical character, is engaging the attention of all branches of evangelical churches, and we were not disappointed ; independent, logical, new in modes of thought and clothing; starting objections and then meeting them ; putting the plough share under beaten definitions and phraseology, but turning up at las thoroughly Wesleyan furrows, so that while the old dress was laid asid you felt safe that the thing itself would take no harm—some of his pos tions, doubtless will awaken discussion and when the request (whic was almost simultaneously made by both preachers and people) fo the publication of the sermon shall be granted, we expect a lively time The best evidence of the scripturality of the discourse is the fact tha numbers of souls entered into the rest of faith while he was preaching. —*The Methodist.*

"The application of the subject is rich in thought and style, an must have thrilled those who heard it."—*Western Advocate.*

"That sermon was the means, under God, of scattering the dar clouds from my mind, and bringing me into the full liberty of the chi dren of God."—*Rev. W. H. Adams.*

"It cleared up some knotty points which had troubled me."—*Rev. (Whitney.*

"I have never read or heard a sermon in which this great and in portant doctrine, in its various bearings, is so concisely and clearly d fined. I feel that I have reached anchorage ground."—*Rev. G. H. Coo sell.*

"It is rich and profound in thought and deeply spiritual."—*Rev. J Vinton.*

"I think it among the best on the subject."—*Rev. A. D. Pulling.*

"The right, and to my mind, the only defensible theory; but the lin is so new, involving so many other doctrines, that only a most caref plan can save from a labyrinth of discussion."—*Rev. F. Bottome, D.1*

"I have been as much pleased and profited in reading as I was hearing it."—*Rev. J. W. Horne, D. D.*

"The point of excellence in the discourse, as it appears to me, its solution of the question as to the relation of regenerate souls no sanctified. I have read about every thing in print on this subject, b have never seen a satisfactory explanation until now."—*Rev. A. I Crawford, A. M.*

"Decidedly the best thing we have ever seen on the doctrine Holiness."—*World's Crisis.*

"The single points of the obliteration of evil habits and the enti sanctification of the soul by the revolutionary and supernatural substit

tion of the Holy Spirit, in opposition to the work of self-determining will alone, is worth more than volumes that have been written on the theme. Indeed we know of no point made in Wesley, Watson, or any other author, of equal value on that head. That alone, the heart and core of the sermon, is of unspeakable value, were there nothing else to preserve. But there are many other excellences of great merit, and the keen analysis, searching logic, forcibleness of thought and statement, and freshness and power of illustration, mark their possessor, we hesitate not to say, as one of the most philosophic minds of the Church, while the unmistakable and baptized unction that pervades the discourse cannot fail to impart its fragrance to every devout reader."—*George Lansing Taylor, D. D.*

"It is admirably stated and conclusive. A very valuable aid to the practical theology of the great doctrine."—*Christian Advocate.*

"I have in it more positive and satisfactory ideas concerning this all-important subject than ever before."—*Rev. S. K. Smith, A. M.*

"It is a power for good."—*Rev. R. H. Wilkinson.*

CHRISTIAN HOLINESS: ITS PHILOSOPHY, THEORY AND EXPERIENCE.

This volume contains all the points of excellence commended in the sermon, together with the results of the author's investigations during the intervening years.

It is believed to be the *only* work upon the subject claiming to be a thorough philosophy constructed according to the scientific method of modern thought.

It is also, like all the author's writings, intensely practical.

304 pp., 16mo, $1. Cloth.

THE HOPE PUBLISHING CO.,

9 DE BEVOISE PLACE, BROOKLYN, N. Y.

www.ingramcontent.com/pod-product-compliance
Lightning Source LLC
Chambersburg PA
CBHW022019240426
43667CB00042B/948